Crownies Of Lowestoft

by Malcolm White

Coastal and Maritime Heritage Series

2000

INFORMATION

Published by	Malcolm R. White, 71 Beeching Drive, Denes Park, Lowestoft, Suffolk, NR32 4TB England, United Kingdom.	Printed by	Micropress Printers Ltd., 27 Norwich Road, Halesworth, Suffolk, IP19 8BX, England, United Kingdom.

First Published October 2000

ISBN 0 9532485 3 4

Front Cover Photograph
GY336 Bellona arrives home from a fishing trip. She joined the Lowestoft fleet in January 1954.

Title page Photograph
After passing through Lowestoft swing bridge, *LT161 King Richard* makes for the pier heads and sea.

Opposite Page Photograph
The *Valeria,* was built for the Arctic Steam Fishing Co. Ltd. in 1898 as *GY818.* She was transferred to Lowestoft in 1924, and in 1925 became *LT156.* On the 18th August 1940, she sank 8 miles from The Smalls after being bombed by enemy aircraft. This scene was recorded on the 26th August 1930, as she left Lowestoft on a fishing trip.

Note
Every effort has been made to ensure the information in this book is accurate. For this reason, official documentation backed up by various research works, and local records have been consulted for factual support. However, when considering such a complex, variable and historical subject, with some material attributable to other parties, 100% accuracy cannot be guaranteed.

CONTENTS

ACKNOWLEDGEMENTS	4
INTRODUCTION	7
THE COMPANY AND THE LOWESTOFT OPERATION	8
TRAWLER IDENTITY CHANGES	12
PHOTOGRAPHIC REVIEW	14
DETAILS OF VESSELS OPERATED FROM LOWESTOFT	44
AT SEA WITH CONSOLIDATED	69
SELECT BIBLIOGRAPHY	71
PHOTOGRAPHIC INDEX	72

ACKNOWLEDGEMENTS

Sources of information that have enabled this review and comprehensive fleet list to be prepared are many. The great majority of the information has come from various sources of official documentation, research works and projects, the archives of the Port of Lowestoft Research Society (PLRS) and recollections of events from very kind and helpful people.

As with other books in this series, the two principal societies dedicated to preserving and recording, the fishing and general maritime heritage of Lowestoft and the surrounding area have provided support and assistance. These societies are the PLRS, and its sister society, the Lowestoft & East Suffolk Maritime Society (LESMS).

The PLRS aims to compile both a written and photographic record of the vessels and industries connected in any way with the Port of Lowestoft.

The LESMS is responsible for the Lowestoft & East Suffolk Maritime Heritage Museum, which is located in the Sparrows Nest, Lowestoft.

Much appreciated has been the assistance and interest in the project from Mr. Hans Boje, Mr. Stanley Earl, LESMS Chairman Mr. Peter Parker, Mr. Parry Watson, Mr. David White, PLRS Chairman Mr. Alan Page, and my fellow officers of the Society. I am grateful to Mr. John Wells and his staff for help and specialised support in the presentation of numerous historic and rare photographs featured in this book. For editorial support in this series, I am very much indebted to Mr. Stuart Jones BA formerly of CEFAS Laboratory, Lowestoft.

Other books in the Coastal and Maritime Series by Malcolm White . . . . .

DOWN THE HARBOUR 1955-1995
40 years of fishing vessels, owners, the harbour and shipyards at Lowestoft ISBN 09532485 0 X

A CENTURY OF FISHING
Fishing from Gt.Yarmouth and Lowestoft ISBN 09532485 1 8

FISHING WITH DIVERSITY
A portrait of the Colne Group of Lowestoft ISBN 09532485 2 6

Web Site: www.MaritimeLowestoft.co.uk E-mail: Books@MaritimeLowestoft.co.uk

LT319 Gunton leaves the Trawl Dock for sea. Columbus Buildings, the offices of the Company at Lowestoft, and bearing the company name are in the background. *Gunton* was built in 1917 as *HMT John Cowarder*, and was purchased by Consolidated in 1923. She was sold to Aberdeen in 1955.

GY11 King Arthur was built in 1899 at Grimsby by Schofield, Hagerup and Doughty. In 1922, she was transferred to Lowestoft and became *LT157 King Charles*. During 1941, she was sold to Boston Deep Sea Fishing & Ice Co. Ltd. and left the Lowestoft fleet. *King Charles* is seen here shortly after passing through the swing bridge on her way to sea. In 1950, she was sold for scrapping.

Introduction

The sight of a steam trawler ploughing through the water with smoke billowing from her funnel has long disappeared. These sturdy, seaworthy and hard working vessels, remembered for their superbly balanced lines, characteristic smells, the sizzling and hissing of steam and water, and clanking winches and engines have passed into history with little to remind us of them. They made a major contribution to the development of the fishing industry and many will say that these vessels made the British fishing industry the greatest in the world. In spite of the hundreds that fished from the major fishing ports of the British Isles not one commercial steam trawler has been preserved.

For many years, the **Consolidated Steam Fishing and Ice Co., (Grimsby), Ltd**., later to become **Consolidated Fisheries Ltd.,** was one of the largest operators of these vessels in this country. Essentially a Grimsby based concern, this book only considers the large fleet of Consolidated Fisheries vessels that from 1920 until 1955 were based at Lowestoft. Apart from one diesel trawler delivered late in the history of the Lowestoft operation, this major trawler fleet was steam powered. In peacetime, it was responsible for the majority of the white fish landed at the port.

As with previous works in this series, this book is intended as a specialised fishing and maritime heritage publication, and it is assumed that the reader has an appreciation of British fishing vessels and the fishing industry. Imperial measures continue to be used throughout.

Locally, much has been written about the fishing industry. This has tended to concentrate on the high profile seasonal herring fishing which relied substantially for success, on the vast visiting Scottish drifter fleets. Trawlers and trawling, the backbone of the industry in the 20th century, have been somewhat neglected, and one of the greats of the British trawling industry, the Consolidated, has been largely ignored. This book seeks to remedy that situation.

Malcolm White
Lowestoft
September 2000

Consolidated Fisheries Ltd.

ORIGINS AND OVERVIEW OF THE GROUP

Within the British fishing industry, Consolidated was one of the big names in the trawling world, and one of the most respected of firms. The Company was formed in the early years of the last century, and was brought about by the merging or "consolidation" of several Grimsby based interests. These primarily consisted of companies set up by, or with which Mr. Emil Hagerup and Mr. George Doughty were involved.

Towards the end of the 19th Century, Hagerup and Doughty were running a coal business and, in 1896, they decided to form and run a trawler owning company. A period of major expansion quickly followed with a large number of trawlers being built for the new Company. By the end of 1899, Hagerup and Doughty had formed a business relationship with James Schofield of Hull, a shipbuilding company. The demand for ships at that time was considerable, and the move into shipbuilding was seen as having endless business possibilities. This new shipbuilding partnership of Schofield, Hagerup & Doughty was responsible for building 15 trawlers. These were placed in the ownership of a second, newly formed Hagerup and Doughty fishing company, the Monarch Steam Fishing Co. Ltd.

Other businesses set up in Grimsby by Hagerup and Doughty included an ice and cold storage company. As occasionally happens, very rapid expansion in business can cause financial problems, and the associated companies started to suffer. In 1901, Mr John D. Marsden J.P. (later Sir John D. Marsden Bart.), was introduced to the trade and played a large part in the stabilisation, and later development of the business.

During 1906, the Consolidated Steam Fishing and Ice Co., (Grimsby), Ltd., was formed by merging companies which included Hagerup, Doughty & Co. Ltd., Monarch Steam Fishing Co. Ltd., Hagerup, Doughty Ice and Cold Storage Co. Ltd. and Schofield, Hagerup & Doughty Ltd.

The expansion of the Company's fishing interests saw new offices opened and fleets established at Lowestoft and Swansea.

In 1927, the name was changed to Consolidated Fisheries Ltd. By this time, over 75 vessels had joined the fleet. These included 32 trawlers, and many of them were of the "Strath" class, built for the Admiralty for naval service during the First World War. After the end of hostilities, a large number of these vessels were disposed of to fishing companies.

THE LOWESTOFT CONNECTION

At the time when Consolidated moved part of their Grimsby fleet to Lowestoft, sailing trawlers were still responsible for much of the trawling from the port. Prior to the arrival of the Company, steam trawlers operating from Lowestoft had met with only limited financial success. In many cases, these vessels were sold after a relative short period of time operating from the port. There were numerous reasons for this; the predominant one being high running costs resulting in poor trading results. As we shall see, due to good forward planning and economic house-keeping, the Consolidated Steam Fishing and Ice Co. Ltd. and it's successor, did much to prevent these two factors affecting the successful running of their Lowestoft operation.

Apart from running a small shipwrights business at Lowestoft since 1918, Consolidated had no major presence at the port until 1920. The first manager at Lowestoft was Mr. George A. Frusher. During 1920, a number of vessels were transferred to Lowestoft from the Grimsby fleet, including many old "fleeters" of the wheelhouse aft type. This type of trawler was designed and built at a time when working in a fleeting and boxing system was common. This involved many similar vessels of the same company working on the fishing grounds under the command of an "admiral". He would give orders to the fleet when to shoot and when to haul, and generally directed the operations of all the vessels. The fleeting system allowed the trawlers to remain at sea for up to eight weeks at a time. Their catches were packed in boxes and transferred by small boat to a fast carrier vessel which would take the fish as speedily as possible to market. Lowestoft trawlers did not work this method of fishing.

Many of the early vessels, which moved to Lowestoft, came from the Hagerup and Doughty, and Monarch fleets. These vessels had almost reached the end of their working lives when they arrived at the port. Rather than try to dispose of them at a time of recession, Consolidated saw new possibilities working them from Lowestoft. With better fishing grounds nearer to the port than at Grimsby, a substantial reduction in running costs was anticipated, together with good landings.
The old "fleeters" generally appeared low in the water, especially when they were just out from port, with full bunkers. After a fishing trip during which he had experienced continuous bad weather, a skipper of one of the Lowestoft based Consolidated "fleeters", remarked: "We dived at the harbour entrance outward bound, and surfaced again at the entrance inward bound!"

The first vessel to be transferred from Grimsby was *GY123 Ashton* on the 2nd October 1920, with *GY178 Ipswich* and *GY358 Oldham* following on the 4th, and *GY266 Scarborough* on the 5th. By the end of 1920, the following trawlers had also arrived at their new home port, *GY129 Aberdeen, GY153 Derby, GY426 Exeter, GY428 Falmouth, GY166 Fleetwood, GY450 Ilfracombe, GY232 Newhaven, GY671 Valentia* and *GY424 Whitby.* Several more vessels were brought south from the Humber during 1921, and others were added from time to time, either by transferring from Grimsby, or by buying them from other owners. In later years, many of these were replacements for those that had been sold, transferred to Swansea or Grimsby, or scrapped. Some of the additions included a number of "Strath" class trawlers built during or just after, the First World War for the Admiralty.

The names of the trawlers making up the Consolidated fleet at Lowestoft generally reflected their original owner. The "King" trawlers, such as *King Henry* and *King Canute* came from Monarch Steam Fishing and the "Town" and "City" named vessels, such as *Fleetwood* and *Leeds*, from Hagerup and Doughty.

With the Consolidated Steam Fishing & Ice Company being in 1926 the largest trawler owner at Lowestoft, the Company's demand for coal was substantial. During the prolonged coal strike their manager; Mr. George Frusher fitted out a large trawler, the *King Canute,* to fetch coal from Ostend. One of the Company's trawler skippers, Billy Mullender, was given command of her.

Billy first went to sea in 1914, as cook on his father's sailing smack. Since the war made it virtually impossible to fish out of Lowestoft, they fished from Padstow. By the time he was 19, he had gained his mate's certificate, and at 21, his skipper's certificate. At 24, he gained his extra skipper's certificate. Billy Mullender's first command was the *Primula,* a sailing trawler, later fitted with an engine. The experiment to ship coal to Lowestoft was so successful that after the strike, the Company decided to ship their own coal from Blyth, in Northumberland, to Lowestoft permanently. Consolidated bought a 1901 built collier, which was renamed the *George Frusher.* "They are putting up a monument to me before I die," said George at the time. Skipper Billy Mullender was given the command of the vessel.

With a steam trawler fleet of around 40 vessels operating from Lowestoft, one collier was soon found inadequent to satisfy the demand. The Company then bought another collier, the *Mons*, and George Frusher gave command of that vessel also to Billy. He would bring one loaded collier from Blyth to Lowestoft, unload, steam back light, and then take over the other one, which had been loading and bring her back. Billy was up and down the coast, turn and turn about, with the *George Frusher* and the *Mons* for 12 years. In one year, they shipped 80,000 tons of coal.
Another operation set up by Consolidated was the bringing of ice to Lowestoft by various vessels of the fleet, including the Grimsby fleet, for use by Lowestoft based trawlers on fishing trips. By supplying coal and ice, the Company substantially reduced the running costs and overheads of the fleet.

Complete with the crown on the funnel, inherited from the Monarch Steam Fishing Co. Ltd., the Consolidated steam trawler was outwardly majestic, tough and proud. Company vessels such as the *Fritton* and *Loddon* were frequently the top earners at Lowestoft. However, life on a steam trawler was not a bed of roses and many of those who crewed these vessels told of rat infestation, smelly, dirty and depressing conditions, very little comfort, and extremely basic washing and toilet facilities.

Requisitioned for war service in both World Wars, many of the Company trawlers were in the front line undertaking Anti-submarine and Minesweeping duties, and in use as examination, patrol, boom defence and escort vessels. Unfortunately, some vessels were lost with a substantial loss of life.

During 1939, the *Fritton* undertook an experimental fishing trip to the Faroe grounds. She landed at Lowestoft on the 19th April, and despite having a good catch, the quality of the fish was not the usual high standard expected at Lowestoft. The prices reflected this, and the case for further trips to these grounds was reconsidered.

The Consolidated trawlers working out of Lowestoft were involved in a number of notable rescues. One example occurred in January 1932, when the *Bellerophon,* under Skipper W. Bridge went to the aid of the Faversham ketch *Rhodesia,* which was disabled and in serious trouble in 65mph winds. With great difficulty, the ketch was towed to safety by the trawler. Without the assistance of the *Bellerophon,* the ketch and possibly her crew, could have been lost. This is just one incident of many, involving trawlers undertaking dangerous missions, which after a very short time, tend to get forgotten.

Generally, Consolidated were considered a very good employer, and looked after its employees well. The annual dinner was always well attended and much appreciated. This was held for many years on New Years Eve at the Great Eastern Hotel, in Denmark Road, Lowestoft.

In 1951, a major policy change by the Company occurred. In that year, the building of the first diesel powered trawler for the Lowestoft Consolidated fleet was completed at the Lowestoft shipyard of Richards Ironworks. This vessel was the *Vanessa Ann,* a 103-foot trawler powered by a 540hp British Polar diesel engine. Many thought that she marked the beginning of a new era, and the modernisation of the ageing Consolidated steam trawler fleet at the port.

Unfortunately this optimism was short lived. In February 1955, the Lowestoft manager, Mr. R. A. Long announced that Consolidated Fisheries were closing their Lowestoft office and would transfer the *Vanessa Ann* to Grimsby. The remaining seven steam trawlers would be laid up. This decision was received with deep regret on the Lowestoft Market. Consolidated were looked upon as an old friend, who had always had a large fleet, ensured consistent landings, attracted the right type of trawlerman and landed a very large proportion of the quality white fish which the merchants liked to buy. "They have always been a good firm to do business with"; commented one well established Lowestoft fish merchant. Another personality, prominent on the market for over 40 years, said that for a great many years, fish merchants would have had little business in white fish had it not been for the great fleet of trawlers belonging to Consolidated. Of the seven steam trawlers, the *Gunton* and *Loddon* were sold to Aberdeen, and continued to fish for a few more years. After a period at North Quay, the other five, *Bellona, Boreas, Erillus, Fritton,* and *Witham* were all sold for scrapping. The sole diesel trawler was later sold to Fleetwood. Eventually she was converted into a sailing ship and is still in service. The Company had only been involved with the trawling side of the industry, during the 35 years it had been at the port

For the majority of their time at Lowestoft, Consolidated occupied Columbus Buildings, an impressive building facing the Trawl Dock. For a few years prior to moving into Columbus Buildings, the Lowestoft office of the Company had been situated at the Consolidated works and stores complex in Commercial Road, not far from the Dry Dock. Columbus Buildings was built in 1907 by Mr. Harry Adams. The Consolidated took over the building in 1926 when three emblems, a crown, a castle and a bull, were added to the front of it. These emblems represented the three companies which had merged to form the Consolidated Company. It is not generally known that Columbus Buildings, was one of the first, if not the first, building with a steel construction in Lowestoft. The building was steel framed, very much a rarity in those days. Designed by Mr. R. Scott Cockrell, the top of the facade was built consisting of glazed earthenware blocks and slabs, representing the ships of Columbus. The ground floor of this unique building was renovated and altered in 1951. The area had been used as a marine store with a net making establishment above. Involved in the work was the removal of the rather unattractive shop fronts, with their boarded windows. The architects, who designed the new ground floor, Messrs. Taylor & Green, were at some pains to see that the original character of the building was not destroyed.
After all the renovation work was completed, Columbus and his fleet still sailed on overhead, and despite its most modern

appearance the ground floor blended well with the older portion of the facade. The building was vacated by Consolidated in 1955, and became the office of Boston Deep Sea Fisheries Ltd. Currently it is the headquarters of Putford Enterprises Ltd., a major operator of standby and supply vessels. The Lowestoft based Boston Putford Offshore Safety group is also based in the building.

During their time at Lowestoft, Consolidated had involvement in a number of properties in the town, in addition to those already mentioned. They had premises on North Quay, initially used as a marine engineering base, but by 1947, in use by the fish merchant side of the business. A small office also existed on the Trawl Market for many years. In the late 1940s, the Company entered into a partnership agreement with the fish-curing firm of J. Clayburn & Co. Ltd., who had a curing yard in Roman Road. However, by the early 1950s, Consolidated Fisheries were concentrating on the core business of trawler owning, and only Columbus Buildings and the works in Commercial Road remained.

Ironically, the transferring of Consolidated Group trawlers from Grimsby to Lowestoft was to be repeated again much later in the 20th century, for in 1978, eleven vessels arrived at Lowestoft. The Company had decided to sell their last trawlers at Grimsby, and the Colne group of companies purchased these. As with the steam trawlers in the 1920s, the vessels *Aldershot, Barnsley, Blackburn Rovers, Carlisle, Crystal Palace, Gillingham, Huddersfield Town, Notts Forest, Port Vale* and *Spurs* soon became familiar names at their new home port. Some resumed their fishing careers working from Lowestoft and others became standby vessels. *Real Madrid,* the other vessel purchased by Colne Shipping at the time, was stripped of valuable components and then sold for scrap. All were diesel "Footballers", a very well known class of vessel within the British fishing industry. After the departure of these trawlers from Grimsby, Consolidated Fisheries Ltd. was left with a fleet of seiners there. At the end of November 1982, it was announced that Consolidated Fisheries Ltd. would cease trading, with the loss of at least 60 jobs at Grimsby. The reasons given were numerous and included the lack of Government help to the industry, poor fishing opportunities for their large trawlers, shortage of cash, withdrawal of bank support, and the failure of a take over bid.

During the following month, Consolidated Fisheries announced the sale of their remaining vessels. The end had finally come for the Company, and another major British fishing concern had ceased trading, and gone out of business forever.
Over the years, the Consolidated Fisheries Group has become legendary in the history of the British fishing industry. In addition to being one of the major British fishing companies, for many years it owned the largest fleet of trawlers at Lowestoft, and was the backbone of the local fishing industry. Although many other firms operated steam trawlers and drifter/trawlers from the port, the presence of the Consolidated is still missed by many who can remember the great days of the British steam trawler fleets, and the many supporting industries that were built up around them

At the start of the 21st century, Lowestoft remains a major trawling port. Today's beam trawlers are very different to the steam trawlers of 50 years ago. However, the present fleet continues the tradition set by the steam and other trawlers before them. All have supplied the market with the superb prime whitefish for which Lowestoft is renowned.

Consolidated Skippers - December 1938.

J. Barber	W. Besford.	F. Bloomfield
J. Blyth	E. Bridge	J. Bridge
W. Bridge Jnr.	W. Bridge Snr	W. Burgoyne
A. Challis	W. Challis	E. Chilvers
T. Chilvers	F. Church	T. Claxton
E. Coleman	H. Cook	J. Dale
A. Durrant	C. Dyer	R. Fryer
J. Gamble	H. Head	H. Hunter
C. Larter	A. Lockwood	A. Muffett *
E. J. Mullender	R. Mullender	H. Norman
J. Nunn	J. Pickess	J. Silom
A. Simpson	W. Spalding	W. Spore
W. Turrell	E. Ward	W. Warford
E. White	G. Wright	J. Wright
	J. E. Wright	

**Company Top Skipper for 1938*

Earlier well known Company skippers include Harrison, Last, Mingay, Musk, Oldman, Reeves and Welch.

Consolidated Fisheries Steam Trawlers

Changes in Identity - Lowestoft Fleet

REGISTRATION AT LOWESTOFT	REGISTRATION ON ARRIVAL	NAME AT LOWESTOFT	NAME ON ARRIVAL	TIME IN FLEET
GY 153	Same	Derby	Same	1920-24
GY 166	Same	Fleetwood	Same	1920
GY 168	Same	Grimsby	Same	1921-22
GY 206	Same	Kingston	Same	1921-22
GY 234	Same	Erillus	Same	1954-55
GY 283	Same	Witham	Same	1939-55
GY 336	Same	Bellona	Same	1954-55
GY 381	Same	Kuvera	Same	1929-33
GY 524	Same	Whitby	Same	1920-22
GY 538	Same	Oldham	Same	1920-22
GY1315	Same	Arlette	Same	1935-36
GY1335	Same	Flavia	Same	1929-35
GY1329	Same	Sabina	Same	1930-33
Lowestoft	GY1124	King Canute	Same	1922-26
LT 84	GY1344	Croton	Same	1935-41
LT 93	HL38	Dover	Same	1924-36
LT 94	GY 391	Jonquil	Same	1935-53
LT 95	WY106	Eastward Ho!	Same	1924-36
LT 96	GY 348	Yulan	Same	1935-45
LT 97	GY 302	Wistaria	Same	1935-39
LT 97	WY59	Grimenco	Same	1925-26
LT 98	GY1087	Brent	Same	1924-35
LT107	GY 311	Ostrich	Same	1924-53
LT109	GY 223	Dahlia	Same	1935-38
LT113	GY1049	Eudocia	Same	1924-41
LT114	GY 126	Adrian	Same	1924-53
LT117	GY 402	Gardenia	Same	1935-39
LT118	GY 605	Zonia	Same	1936-41
LT121	GY 123	Ashton	Same	1920-28
LT123	GY 129	Aberdeen	Same	1920-37
LT128	GY 178	Ipswich	Same	1920-41
LT131	GY 207	Leeds	Same	1924-41
LT134	GY 232	Newhaven	Same	1920-40
LT135	GY 255	Richmond	Same	1921-27
LT136	GY 266	Scarborough	Same	1920-37
LT138	GY 330	Xania	Same	1921-37
LT139	GY 426	Exeter	Same	1920-29

REGISTRATION AT LOWESTOFT	REGISTRATION ON ARRIVAL	NAME AT LOWESTOFT	NAME ON ARRIVAL	TIME IN FLEET
LT143	GY 428	Falmouth	Same	1920-38
LT144	GY 442	Halifax	Same	1921-40
LT148	GY 450	Ilfracombe	Same	1920-37
LT150	GY 568	Valentia	Same	1920-38
LT153	GY 671	Rochester	Same	1920-41
LT154	GY 760	Zetland	Same	1924-36
LT156	GY 818	Valeria	Same	1924-40
LT157	GY 11	King Charles	King Arthur	1922-41
LT160	GY 97	King Athelstan	King Egbert	1923-53
LT161	GY1181	King Richard	Same	1925-53
LT169	GY1195	King Edward	Same	1923-53
LT170	GY 339	Bucentaur	Same	1922-47
LT173	GY 151	Zodiac	Same	1925-33
LT180	H111	Volta	Same	1925-38
LT184	H169	Ampere	Same	1925-39
LT187	H177	Fidelia	Same	1925-41
LT248	GY1146	Dereham	Rinto	1938-54
LT252	GY1208	Framlingham	Rodrigo	1938-44
LT265	GY1233	Rendlesham	Rosareno	1938-40
LT274	GY1232	Lavenham	Rosco	1938-43
LT279	GY 23	Walsingham	Renovo	1938-39
LT286	GY 22	Saxmundham	Roto	1938-45
LT297	GY1337	Fritton	Ninette	1930-55
LT301	GY 270	Belton	River Tummel	1938-40
LT309	GY 272	Loddon	River Kelvin	1938-55
LT317	GY 276	Hopton	River Findhorn	1938-41
LT319	GY 289	Gunton	River Nith	1938-55
LT320	GY 291	Flixton	River Orchy	1938-43
LT326	H383	City of Aberdeen	Same	1927-43
LT355	GY1169	King Henry	Same	1925-41
LT396	GY 335	Bellerophon	Same	1922-46
LT398	GY 338	Boreas	Same	1927-55
LT406	H483	Shamrock	Same	1928-45
LT408	A300	Thistle	Same	1928-36
LT410	A393	Wolseley	Same	1928-44

Note

Upon transfer to Lowestoft, some trawlers retained their previous identity. Others underwent a change in identity after a few years at the port. Many however, were given new registrations, and in some cases new names, soon after transfer.

Previously registered at North Shields, Grimsby and Aberdeen, *LT410 Wolseley* was transferred to Lowestoft in 1924. She is seen here entering the Waveney Dock.

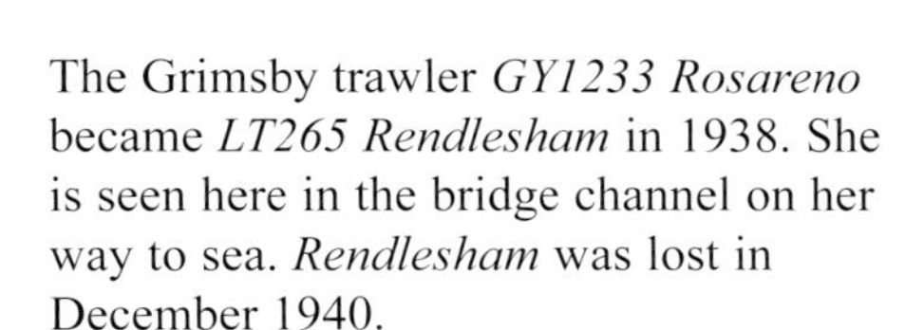

The Grimsby trawler *GY1233 Rosareno* became *LT265 Rendlesham* in 1938. She is seen here in the bridge channel on her way to sea. *Rendlesham* was lost in December 1940.

(Above) Four lads fishing using handlines, watch as *LT170 Bucentaur* arrives home and a Lowestoft drifter leaves for the herring grounds. Previously *GY339*, the *Bucentaur* was lost with all hands in May 1947. It is assumed she sank after being in collision with the *Wilson Victory*.

(Right) Consolidated Fisheries trawlers laid up in the mid 1930s at the "The Crick" in the Inner Harbour.

One of many products from the Mackie & Thomson yard in the Consolidated fleet was *LT118 Zonia.* She was previously *GY605 Apollo* and later *GY227 Zonia*. Other registrations carried by her include *DO88* and *GY139*. She was sold for scrapping in 1950.

LT160 King Athelstan was built for Monarch Steam Fishing as *GY97 King Egbert*. She changed her identity in the mid 1920s. This view shows her leaving Lowestoft on the 4th October 1928. During April 1953 she was sold for scrapping.

In the mid 1920s, the trawler *King Canute* was refitted to enable her to carry coal from Belgium to Lowestoft for use by the steam trawlers of the Consolidated fleet.

Still very much a trawler, but in use as a collier, *GY1124 King Canute* approaches the pier heads at Lowestoft in 1926.

On the 4th October 1927, the *King Canute,* by now stripped of her fishing capability, heads into Lowestoft with a cargo of coal. At the time, she was officially classed as a cargo steamer.

Transferred to Lowestoft in 1920, *LT123 Aberdeen* was built as *GY 129 Aberdeen* for Hagerup and Doughty in 1896 by Mackie & Thomson, at Govan . She was sold to Milford Haven owners in 1937, and was lost in Cardigan Bay, following an attack by enemy aircraft on 11th March 1941.

LT *169 King Edward* is seen entering the Trawl Dock on return from a fishing trip. She was built as *GY1195* at Grimsby in 1899, and was sold for scrapping in April 1953.

One of the three coasters operated from Lowestoft by Consolidated, the *Mons* was built as the *Southminster* in 1919. She was sold in 1940.

Of the vessels transferred to Lowestoft in 1920, many retained their Grimsby registrations for several years. One of these vessels, *GY178 Ipswich, is* seen here entering the port in 1924. She gained the Lowestoft registration *LT 128* in 1925. Sold in 1941, she later became *H56. Ipswich* was broken up at Grays, Essex in 1953.

The Inner Harbour on 30th January 1939, and *LT279 Walsingham* is being made ready for sea. She was orginally *GY23 Renovo* and had transferred to Lowestoft in 1938. *Walsingham* was lost following a collision in 1941.

(Above) It is the morning of 3rd October 1930, and having just passed through Lowestoft swing bridge, the 1897 built *LT 136 Scarborough* heads for sea. She was previously registered *GY266*, and is here passing a Banff steam drifter in the bridge channel.

(Right) Just home from a fishing trip, *LT252 Framlingham* makes for her berth in the Waveney Dock on 16th August 1939. Within a few months, she was to be extensively damaged when attacked by an enemy aircraft. She was later sold, and eventually broken up in 1952.

(Above) Photographs of Lowestoft steam trawlers at Great Yarmouth are quite rare. In this view, we see the 1904 built *LT286 Saxmundham* on a visit to the port. She joined the Lowestoft fleet in 1938 and was previously *GY22 Roto*. During 1952, *Saxmundham* was sold for scrapping.

(Right) A classic photograph showing the crew of a Consolidated trawler assembled in front of the trawl winch. The vessel is *LT157 King Charles*, previously *GY11 King Arthur*. Mr. B. Austrin, whose father is the chap on the extreme right, kindly supplied this photograph for inclusion in this book. The chap in the centre with the collar and tie is possibly Skipper White.

The *Eastward Ho! was* built in 1898 as *H415* for S. T. White & Co. Ltd. She was sold in 1920, and registered as *WY106. Eastward Ho!* joined the Lowestoft Consolidated fleet in 1924, and became *LT95* in 1925. She was sold for scrapping in 1936.

(Right) Seen here entering Lowestoft as *GY671,* the *Rochester* gained her Lowestoft registration of *LT153* in 1925. She was a totalloss in July 1944, after being mined.

Built in 1891 at Canning Town, *LT96 Yulan* was powered by a 45hp Amos & Smith triple expansion engine. She was initially registered *GY348*. *Yulan* was sold in 1945, and after a number of ownership changes, she was scrapped in 1948 at Great Yarmouth.

It is the morning of the 28th September 1928, and *LT355 King Henry* heads out of Lowestoft into a fresh north easterly breeze, on her way to the fishing grounds. She was built in 1900 at Grimsby and was previously *GY1169*. On the 13th June 1941, *King Henry* was sunk during one of the many German air attacks on Lowestoft

In 1938, *LT143 Falmouth* was sold to Pair Fishing, and registered as *M286*. She had joined the fleet in 1920, and was registered *LT143* in 1925. Her original registration was *GY428*. *Falmouth* was lost in 1945, after being mined. This print is from the Maritime Photo Library Collection.

The *Leeds* joined the Lowestoft fleet in 1924, and during the following year became *LT 131*. She was built in 1897 at Govan, and her original registration was *GY207*. *Leeds* was sold for scrapping in 1950.

The *Fleetwood* was officially transferred by Consolidated to Lowestoft in early October 1920. By the end of November 1920, she had become a total loss on the Scroby Sands off Great Yarmouth after grounding. *Fleetwood* never did receive her Lowestoft registration, keeping her Grimsby registration of *GY166,* to the end. She is seen here earlier in her life at Grimsby.

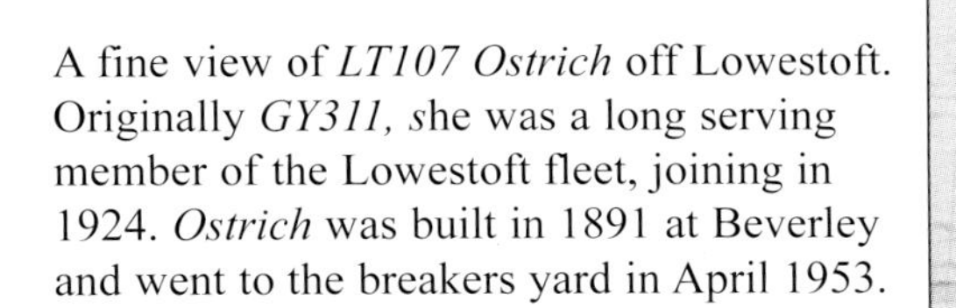

A fine view of *LT107 Ostrich* off Lowestoft. Originally *GY311, s*he was a long serving member of the Lowestoft fleet, joining in 1924. *Ostrich* was built in 1891 at Beverley and went to the breakers yard in April 1953.

The first of the three colliers to be acquired by the Company and be based at Lowestoft, was *George Frusher*. Previously the *Carlston,* the vessel was purchased in 1927. She is seen here on the 18th September 1928, arriving at Lowestoft with a cargo of coal for the fleet.

Purchased by Consolidated in 1925 for their Lowestoft fleet, the *Ampere* was originally *H169* and owned by F. & T. Ross Ltd. She became *LT184* at Lowestoft and was sold in 1939. *Ampere* left Lowestoft for Antwerp in February of that year. We see her here heading out of Lowestoft for the fishing grounds on 30th September 1930.

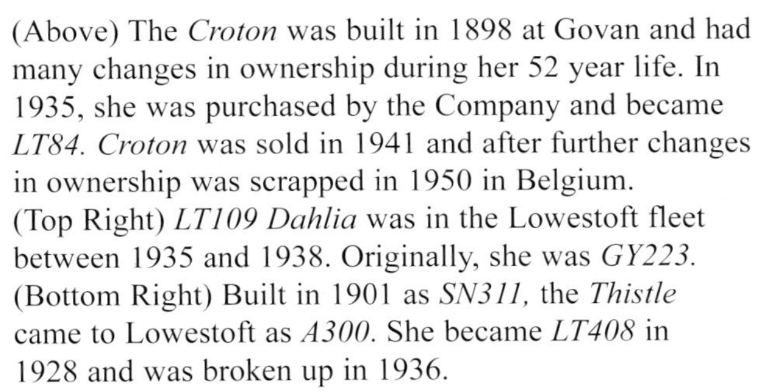

(Above) The *Croton* was built in 1898 at Govan and had many changes in ownership during her 52 year life. In 1935, she was purchased by the Company and became *LT84. Croton* was sold in 1941 and after further changes in ownership was scrapped in 1950 in Belgium.
(Top Right) *LT109 Dahlia* was in the Lowestoft fleet between 1935 and 1938. Originally, she was *GY223.*
(Bottom Right) Built in 1901 as *SN311,* the *Thistle* came to Lowestoft as *A300.* She became *LT408* in 1928 and was broken up in 1936.

The "Strath" class steam trawler *LO319 William Harrison*, formerly *HMT William Harrison,* seen leaving Lowestoft in 1920. Built in 1919 at Wivenhoe, she was purchased in 1921 and became the Consolidated trawler *GY1355 Flavia* (see page 34). During 1935, she was sold to John Craig and moved to Aberdeen, where she received the registration *A373. Flavia* was lost on the 28th August 1940.

(Right) The 1900 built *LT355 King Henry* off Lowestoft. She was transferred to Lowestoft in 1925, and was originally *GY1169*.

(Below) Naval Service in both World Wars saw Consolidated trawlers undertaking many different duties. This rare and historic print shows a requisitioned steam trawler converted for Admiralty use, in the Inner Harbour at Lowestoft. Another requisitioned trawler, the harbour shearlegs, and the Great Eastern Railway paddle tug, the *Despatch*, can be seen.

(Above) A scene in the Inner Harbour in 1938 showing the *Lavenham* and the *Loddon*. *LT274 Lavenham* was built in 1902 as *GY1232 Rosco*. She later transferred to Grimsby and became *GY3*. In 1952, the *Lavenham* was sold for scrap.
(Top Right) The "Strath" class trawler *Fritton* off Lowestoft in the early 1950s. Built in 1918 as *HMT Thomas Dear*, she was sold to Consolidated in 1921, and registered *GY1337*. In 1938, she became *LT297*.
(Bottom Right) Another "Strath", the *Loddon*, seen leaving Lowestoft. Built in 1919 as *HMT George Lane,* and completed as *River Kelvin,* she passed into Consolidated ownership in 1922. She became *GY272 River Kelvin,* and by 1939, was *LT309 Loddon.* She was sold in 1955 to Aberdeen, and continued her fishing career there.

The view from the South Pier at Lowestoft on the 10th October 1930, as *LT406 Shamrock* leaves the port for the fishing grounds. Built as *H483* in 1899 by Cook, Welton & Gemmell, *Shamrock* had her registration changed to *LT406* in 1928, when she joined the Consolidated fleet.

Built in 1897 by Mackie & Thomson at Govan, as *GY232,* the *Newhaven* was transferred to Lowestoft in 1920, and registered as *LT 134* in 1925. On 15th January 1940, she became a total loss after being mined 18miles SSE of her home port. On the 26th October 1937, when this photograph was taken, we find her making her approach to Lowestoft on return from a fishing trip.

The *Valentia,* seen here entering Lowestoft on the afternoon of 18th October 1932, was built at Irvine as *GY568*. She was in the Lowestoft fleet from 1920 until 1938, and during that time, she became *LT150. Valentia* was sold in 1938 to Pair Fishing of Milford Haven. She later passed to Grimsby owners, and in 1949, was sold for scrapping.

GY22 Roto joined the Lowestoft fleet and became *LT286 Saxmundham,* after being purchased by Consolidated in 1938. As *Roto* she was built at Beverley in 1904 for Sir G. F. Sleight and others. After being disposed of by the Company in 1945, *Saxmundham* was owned by the Raw Materials Supply Corporation and later by Cranbrook Shipping. She was sold for scrapping in 1952. This print is from the Maritime Photo Library collection.

Declared a total loss in January 1950, *GY381 Kuvera* was part of the Lowestoft fleet from 1929 until 1933. She was built as *HMT John Heath,* and after leaving Lowestoft, worked from Grimsby and later Aberdeen.

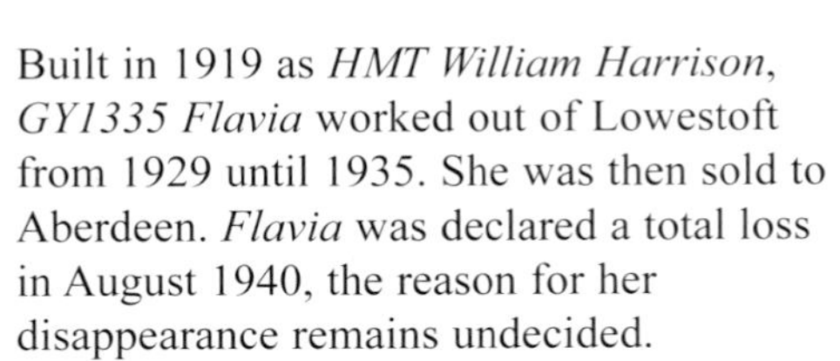
Built in 1919 as *HMT William Harrison, GY1335 Flavia* worked out of Lowestoft from 1929 until 1935. She was then sold to Aberdeen. *Flavia* was declared a total loss in August 1940, the reason for her disappearance remains undecided.

The majority of the trawlers in the Consolidated fleet could be grouped together into a number of standard types or designs.

Many of the wheelhouse aft trawlers were built to the same design by Mackie & Thomson. The fleet included several "Strath" class vessels, built to an Admiralty standard at different yards, and there were a number of other wheelhouse aft trawlers all built to a similar design by Cochrane & Cooper. Examples of another type were the *'Kings' Athelstan, Charles, Edward, Henry* and *Richard,* all built by Schofield, Hagerup & Doughty around 1900.

A particularly handsome batch of trawlers were built in 1907 by Cochrane. These included *Bellerophon, Bellona, Boreas and Bucentaur.* All of these have been included in this book. The *Bellona* is featured on the front cover, and the *Bellerophon* on the back cover. The other two are seen here from the end of the South Pier in 1928, *Bucentaur* on 7th October, and *Boreas* on 23rd September.

(Top Right) Built as *GY338*, the *Boreas* was transferred to Lowestoft in 1927, and became *LT398* in 1928. After many years service, she was sold for scrapping in 1955. *Boreas* was one of the last seven steamers in the Consolidated fleet at the port.

(Bottom Right) *LT170 Bucentaur* was previously *GY339,* and joined the local fleet in 1922. She was lost with all hands following a collision in fog on 21st May 1947. It was assumed that the other vessel involved in the collision was the American steamer *Wilson Victory,* on charter to the United States Army.

This fine view of the newly completed small diesel powered trawler *Rewga,* taken in 1937, appears to have little in common with the subject of this book. Close examination however, reveals aspects of the Consolidated operation at Lowestoft and includes six, possibly seven, of their vessels. In the background on North Quay can be seen, from left to right, the coaster *Mons,* with a trawler alongside, *LT184 Ampere,* and two large Grimsby trawlers, one of which is *GY1041 Franc-Tireur.* To the right of these three vessels, are two wheelhouse aft trawlers, one of which is *LT153 Rochester,* the other is possibly *LT144 Halifax.* The *Franc-Tireur* was lost in 1943, and the *Rochester* in 1944. As mentioned elsewhere, the *Mons* was employed on bringing coal from the northeast, and large Grimsby trawlers were employed on the "ice run" from Grimsby. In the railway sidings, amongst the dozens of coal trucks, a Great Eastern Railway class Y14 locomotive can be seen.

Following their disposal by the Admiralty, Consolidated acquired around thirty "Strath" class trawlers in the 1920s. On this page, three vessels of this type are featured, all displaying Grimsby registrations.

(Right) *GY293 River Leven* made occasional landings at Lowestoft between October 1938 and March 1939. In this view, we find her at anchor in the Humber. She was built in 1918 at Paisley as *HMT John Edsworth.*

(Left) A long serving member of the Lowestoft fleet, the *Witham* retained the Grimsby registration of *GY283,* throughout her time at the port. She was built as *HMT Stephen Kenny* in 1919. *Witham* was requisitioned during the Second World War for use as a minesweeper, and was one of the last trawlers of the great Consolidated Lowestoft fleet to leave, when sold for scrapping in 1955.

(Right) The *River Tummel* was one of five similar vessels transferred to Lowestoft in 1938, named after rivers. Destined to become *LT301 Belton,* she is seen in this view heading out of Lowestoft with her Grimsby registration of *GY270. Belton* was built as *HMT Thomas Foley* in 1918, and served in the Second World War as an examination vessel. She was sold for scrapping in 1955.

The 1897 built *GY255 Richmond*, was one of the 1921 batch of trawlers transferred to Lowestoft. In this poor quality but valuable photograph, she is seen in 1923 entering the port. *Richmond* was registered as *LT135* in 1925, and after three changes of ownership, was scrapped in 1935.

LT248 Dereham, here approaching the harbour entrance, had a long and successful career as part of the Lowestoft trawling fleet. She was built in 1900 at Selby, as *GY1146 Rinto* by Cochrane & Cooper. *Rinto* was acquired in 1938 by Consolidated, after which she was renamed and given her Lowestoft registration. On the 4th May 1954, *Dereham* left Lowestoft for breaking up at Southampton.

George Frusher, the steam coaster purchased in 1927, was sold for scrapping in 1938. To replace her, the Company acquired another more modern vessel, the *Kylebank*. She was built at Middlesborough in 1917 as the *Suffolk Coast*, and purchased by Consolidated in 1939 whereupon she was renamed *East Anglian*. She was owned by the Company until 1946. Her new owner in 1946 renamed her *Sussex Oak* and after nine years service, she was sold for scrapping. The *Kylebank* is seen here in 1939, off Lowestoft, and before being renamed *East Anglian*.

The superb lines of the "Strath" class trawlers are well illustrated in these three views. This type of trawler was well represented in the Company fleet at the port.

The vessel in the top and middle views was built as *HMT Thomas Dear*, at Workington in 1918. The vessel in the bottom view was built as *HMT Thomas Foley,* she was also built in 1918, but at Glasgow.

(Top) As the Grimsby trawler *GY1337 Ninette*, the *Thomas Dear* leaves Lowestoft in the 1930s, accompanied by the pilot boat. In 1938, the *Ninette* became the Lowestoft registered *Fritton.*
(Middle) *LT297 Fritton* was sold for scrap in 1955, after she had became one of the "magnificent seven". This name was given locally to the last seven steam trawlers of the Lowestoft Consolidated fleet. These had worked right up to the closure of the Lowestoft operation. From the extension on the North Pier we find her just clearing the harbour entrance, setting out on another fishing trip in the last years of her life.
(Bottom) *Thomas Foley* became *River Tummel* in 1919 and was acquired by Consolidated in 1923. She became *LT301 Belton* in 1938. Later she was sold to North Shields, and eventually sold for scrapping in 1955.
On her way to sea in July 1939, *Belton* is passing the well known Co-operative Wholesale Society canning factory. As part of a scheme to redevelop the Inner Harbour, this factory was demolished in 2000 to make way for another business park.

The early 1950s saw the remaining Consolidated wheelhouse aft trawlers leave for various breakers yards. In the Inner Harbour, minus their sails, two of these vessels, the *King Edward* and possibly *King Athelstan* are seen in the last few weeks of their lives, being prepared for their final voyage. Also visible is a modern Richards built diesel drifter/trawler, rigged for trawling, and a steam coaster which is either the *St. Abbs Head* or *Barra Head.*

Two additional steam trawlers joined the Lowestoft fleet in 1954. These worked from the port until the closure of the Lowestoft office, when they were both sold for scrapping. The two were *GY336 Bellona* and *GY234 Erillus.* In this fine view the *Erillus* is heading north off Lowestoft, on a calm day with an easterly breeze blowing. She was built in 1914 and was a product of Smith's Dock at Middlesborough. Her engine was the well proven 68hp Smith's Dock triple. On the 21st April 1955, in company with *LT297 Fritton,* she left Lowestoft for Dorkins yard at Gateshead for scrapping.

(Top Left) Final days for *GY283 Witham*. This photograph was taken in 1955, when she was one of the remaining steam trawlers laid up at North Quay, awaiting their fate. *Witham* was sold for scrapping to T. W. Ward & Co. Ltd. at Grays, and left Lowestoft on 5th April 1955.

(Top Right) One of the very last landings by a Company trawler at Lowestoft, was made by *LT319 Gunton*. Here she is seen in the Waveney Dock, after completing that landing.

(Bottom Left) After the cessation of operations at Lowestoft, two of the Consolidated steam trawlers were sold to Aberdeen. These were the *Gunton* and the *Loddon*. In company with four other steam trawlers, *A8 Loddon* leaves for sea as part of the Aberdeen fleet. She was eventually sold for scrapping in 1960.

DETAILS OF VESSELS OPERATED OUT OF LOWESTOFT BY THE CONSOLIDATED STEAM FISHING & ICE CO. LTD., AND THE SUCCEEDING COMPANY BETWEEN 1920-1955

The following log includes fishing and non-fishing vessels which were owned by the Company and operated out of Lowestoft. In some cases a vessel will appear more than once, but with a different identity. A number of other vessels visited the port, but are not considered part of the fleet because of the brief period they had working from Lowestoft. e.g. *GY293 River Leven* made a number of landings in 1938-39.

Explanation of columns

Name — The name carried by the vessel while part of the Lowestoft Consolidated fleet.

Fishing Registration — The registration consisting of port letters and fishing numbers, as carried by the vessel when regularly fishing from Lowestoft. Explanation of the different port registrations can be found below in the "History" section.

Official No. — The official number of the vessel.

Call Sign — The registered radio call sign.

Gross/Net Tonnage — As recorded in official documentation. Given in imperial units.

Dimensions — As recorded in official documentation. Given in imperial units and rounded to nearest foot.

Construction — The type of material used for the construction of the majority of the vessel.

Propulsion/Power Unit — Main engine information. In a very few cases, this was subject to change during the life of the vessel.

Build Date — The year the vessel was built.
Yard — The yard at which the vessel was built.
Location — The location of the yard.

History — Highlights of the vessel's life, including any change in use. Particular emphasis is placed upon the time when she was a Lowestoft registered or based vessel. The date given for the selling or transferring of a vessel may be approximate; this information could have been subject to commercial confidence. Vessels that were His Majesty's Trawlers are identified as HMT. As a general rule, all vessels shown as owned by the Consolidated Steam Fishing & Ice Co. Ltd., were transferred in 1927 into the ownership of Consolidated Fisheries Ltd. This internal change has not been shown in this column. Included in this column are the following port distinguishing letters: -

Letter(s)	Port	Letter(s)	Port
A	Aberdeen	LO	London
DO	Douglas, I.o.M.	LT	Lowestoft
FD	Fleetwood	M	Milford Haven
GY	Grimsby	ME	Montrose
H	Hull	SD	Stromstad (Sweden)
IJM	Ymuiden (Holland)	SN	North Shields
LH	Leith	WY	Whitby

Name/Fishing Registration At Lowestoft	Official No. Call Sign	Gross Tonnage Net Tonnage	Dimensions(ft) Construction	Propulsion Unit/Make	Build Date Build Yard Build Location	History
Aberdeen GY129	106676					For details see below
Aberdeen LT123	106676 GFFW	163 68	104 x 20 x 11 Steel	45hp 3cyl Triple Muir & Houston	1896 Mackie & Thomson Govan	Built as GY129 Aberdeen for Hagerup & Doughty 1906 Transferred to Consolidated S.F. & Ice Co. Ltd. 1914-18 War Service 1920 Transferred to Lowestoft on 22nd October 1925 Registration changed to LT123 1937 Sold to Don Trawling Co. Ltd, Milford Haven 1939 Sold to Pair Fishing Co. Ltd., Milford Haven 1941 Lost after an air attack and bombing in Cardigan Bay on 11th March
Adrian GY129	108474					For details see below
Adrian LT114	108474 MCNN	162 69	100 x 20 x 11 Iron	45hp 3cyl Triple Holmes	1897 Cochrane & Cooper Beverley	Built as GY345 Cormorant for Thos. W. Baskcomb 1910 Sold to Black and Hill 1914 Sold to Savoy Fishing Co. Ltd. 1915 Became SN376 Cormorant IV 1915 In use as a Q ship 1920 Sold to Roulette S. Drifter, Trawler & Fishing Co. Ltd. 1920 Registration to SN376 1922 Sold to Allen & Lambert and renamed Adrian 1924 Sold to Consolidated S. F. & Ice Co. Ltd. 1924 Transferred to Lowestoft on 9th December 1925 Registration changed to LT114 1953 Sold to J. J. King & Co. Ltd, Gateshead, for scrapping 1953 Left Lowestoft with Ostrich in tow on 30th April
Ampere LT184	098766 MCRX	154 61	101 x 20 x 11 Iron	50hp 3cyl Triple Holmes	1891 Cochrane, Cooper & Schofield Beverley	Built as H169 Ampere for F. & T. Ross Ltd., Hull 1925 Sold to Consolidated S. F. & Ice Co. Ltd. 1925 Transferred to Lowestoft on 6th January 1925 Registration changed to LT184 1939 Sold to C. Valkenburg 1939 Left Lowestoft for Antwerp on 10th February

Name/Fishing Registration At Lowestoft	Official No. Call Sign	Gross Tonnage Net Tonnage	Dimensions(ft) Construction	Propulsion Unit/Make	Build Date Build Yard Build Location	History
Arlette GY1315	143467 MCRZ	205 83	115 x 22 x 12 Steel	57hp 3cyl Triple Ross & Duncan	1918 Murdoch & Murray P. Glasgow	Built as HMT George French 1919 Registered as LO197 1921 Sold to Consolidated S. F. & Ice Co. Ltd. 1921 Registration changed to GY1315 1922 Renamed Arlette 1935 Transferred to Lowestoft on 7th November 1936 Transferred to Grimsby on 23rd January 1943 Sold to Sir John Irvine, A. Meekie and others 1952 Transferred to R. Irvin & Sons Ltd. 1955 Sold to Cork for use as a coal carrier 1959 Registry changed to Cork 1959 Sold for scrapping
Ashton GY123	106672					For details see below
Ashton LT121 Ltd.	106672	144 53	104 x 21 x 11 Iron	30hp 3cyl Triple N. E. Marine	1896 Edward Bros. N. Shields	Built as GY123 Ashton for Hagerup & Doughty 1906 Transferred to Consolidated S. F. & Ice Co. 1914-18 War Service 1920 Transferred to Lowestoft on 2nd October 1925 Registration changed to LT121 1928 Sold to Dutch owners during May 1928 Became IJM63 Ecliptica 1930 Sold during August and renamed Juliana 1935 Sold for scrapping during August
Bellerophon GY335	125083					For details see below
Bellerophon LT396	125083 GLVB	184 88	105 x 21 x 11 Steel	57hp 3cyl Triple Holmes	1907 Cochrane Selby	Built as GY335 Bellerophon for Consolidated S. F. & Ice 1914-19 War Service 1915 Renamed Bellerophon II 1922 Transferred to Lowestoft on 13th February 1922 Renamed Bellerophon 1928 Registration changed to LT396 1946 Sold to J. C. Llewellyn, Milford Haven 1946 Transferred to Walton Fishing Co. Ltd. 1954 Sold during April for scrapping

Name/Fishing Registration At Lowestoft	Official No. Call Sign	Gross Tonnage Net Tonnage	Dimensions(ft) Construction	Propulsion Unit/Make	Build Date Build Yard Build Location	History
Bellona GY336	125084 GJBG	184 88	105 x 21 x 11 Steel	57hp 3cyl Triple Holmes	1907 Cochrane Selby	Built for Consolidated S. F. & Ice Co. Ltd. 1914-18 War service 1915 Renamed Bellona II 1919 Renamed Bellona 1939-45 War service as Egeria 1954 Transferred to Lowestoft on 3rd January 1955 Sold to T. W. Ward & Co. Ltd., Grays, for scrapping. 1955 Left Lowestoft for Grays on 11th March
Belton LT301	143768 GDTZ	202 88	116 x 22 x 12 Steel	57hp 3cyl Triple Fairfield	1918 Richie, Graham & Milne Glasgow	Built as HMT Thomas Foley ("Strath" class) 1919 Sold to Montrose Steam Fishing Co. Ltd. 1919 Became ME119 River Tummel 1923 Bought by Consolidated S. F. & Ice Co. Ltd. 1923 Became GY270 River Tummel 1938 Transferred to Lowestoft on 17th November 1938 Became LT301 Belton 1940-45 War service 1943 Sold to R. Irvin & Sons Ltd. 1955 Sold to T. W. Ward & Co. Ltd., Grays, for scrapping
Boreas LT398	125086 GBDJ	184 88	105 x 21 x 11 Steel	57hp 3cyl Triple Holmes	1907 Cochrane Selby	Built as GY338 Boreas for Consolidated S. F. & Ice Co. 1914-18 War Service 1927 Transferred to Lowestoft on 8th December 1928 Registration changed to LT398 1939-40 War service as Cuckoo 1955 Sold to T. W. Ward & Co. Ltd., Grays, for scrapping 1955 Left Lowestoft on 10th March
Brent LT98	093935 MSTW	142 54	100 x 20 x 11 Steel	45hp 3cyl Triple Rowan	1892 W. Hamilton P.Glasgow	Built as Brent for Glasgow owners 1899 Sold to W. Sutherland and Jas. Reid 1899 Registration changed to A62 1917 Sold to T. Langley and others, Grimsby 1917 Registration changed to GY1087 1917 Transferred to Brent Steam Fishing Co. Ltd. 1919 Sold to W. Stringer and others 1924 Sold to C. Russell and B. Robson 1924 Sold to Consolidated S. F. & Ice Co. Ltd. 1924 Transferred to Lowestoft on 30th November 1924 Registration changed to LT98 1935 Sold for scrapping 1935 Left Lowestoft on 15th October

Name/Fishing Registration At Lowestoft	Official No. Call Sign	Gross Tonnage Net Tonnage	Dimensions(ft) Construction	Propulsion Unit/Make	Build Date Build Yard Build Location	History
Bucentaur GY339	125087				For details see below	
Bucentaur LT170	125087	184 88	105 x 21 x 11 Steel	57hp 3cyl Triple Holmes	1907 Cochrane Selby	Built as GY339 Bucentaur for Consolidated S. F. & I. 1914-17 War service 1922 Transferred to Lowestoft on 2nd March 1925 Registration changed to LT170 1939-40 War Service 1947 Lost with all hands in the North Sea on 21st May after collision with SS Wilson Victory
City Of Aberdeen LT326	109009 MQZG	194 75	112 x 21 x 11 Steel	63hp 3cyl Triple Hall	1897 A. Hall Aberdeen	Built as H383 City of Aberdeen for G. S. Bowman 1923 In the ownership of Consolidated S. F. & Ice Co. Ltd. 1927 Transferred to Lowestoft on 20th January 1927 Registration changed to LT326 1939-40 War Service 1943 Sold to Loyal Steam Fishing Co. Ltd. 1943 Registration changed to GY432 1947 Sold to W. Benstone 1950 Sold to H.Wood 1950 Sold for scrapping
Croton LT84	109541	150 58	101 x 20 x 11 Steel	41hp 3cyl Triple Ross & Duncan	1898 Mackie & Thomson Govan	Built as GY716 Croton for Orient S. F. Co. Ltd. 1901 Sold to Norway. Registration changed to SD9. 1914 Sold to Orient S. F. Co. Ltd., Grimsby 1914 Registration changed to GY49 1914-19 War Service 1920 Sold to Direct Fish Supplies 1920 Registration changed to DO89 1922 Sold to T. W. Baskcomb, Grimsby 1922 Registration changed to GY1344 1935 Sold to Consolidated Fisheries Ltd. 1935 Transferred to Lowestoft 1935 Registration changed to LT84 1941 Sold to J. Marr & Son Ltd. 1945 Sold to Partnership (Hull) Ltd. 1945 Sold to Mostyn & Willey Ltd 1950 Sold to shipbreakers in Belgium

Name/Fishing Registration At Lowestoft	Official No. Call Sign	Gross Tonnage Net Tonnage	Dimensions(ft) Construction	Propulsion Unit/Make	Build Date Build Yard Build Location	History
Dahlia LT109	096206 LHDW	156 91	101 x 21 x 11 Iron	50hp 3cyl Triple Holmes	1889 Cochrane, Cooper & Schofield Beverley	Built as GY223 Dahlia for North East S. F. Co. Ltd. 1914-19 War Service 1915 Name changed to Dahlia II 1919 Sold to T. W. Baskcomb 1922 Named changed to Dahlia 1935 Sold to Consolidated Fisheries Ltd. 1935 Transferred to Lowestoft 1935 Registration changed to LT109 1938 Sold to Willebrock, Belgium 1938 Left Lowestoft for scrapping on 6th October
Derby GY153	106683	144 54	104 x 20 x 10 Iron	45hp 3cyl Triple North East Marine	1896 Edward Bros. N. Shields	Built for Hagerup and Doughty 1906 Transferred to Consolidated S. F. & Ice Co. Ltd. 1920 Transferred to Lowestoft on 11th October 1924 Sold to Mauritius 1924 Registry closed
Dereham LT248	110943 GPYW	169 66	101 x 21 x 11 Iron	55hp 3cyl Triple Holmes	1900 Cochrane & Cooper Selby	Built as GY1146 Rinto for Sir G. F. Sleight & others 1914-18 War Service 1933 Transferred to Sleight and Humphreys 1938 Sold to Consolidated Fisheries Ltd. 1938 Transferred to Lowestoft in November 1938 Registration changed to LT248 1939 Renamed Dereham 1954 Sold to British Iron & Steel Corporation Ltd. 1954 Passed to Pollock, Brown & Co. Ltd. for scrapping 1954 Left Lowestoft for Southampton on 4th May
Dover LT93	106681	163 68	104 x 20 x 11 Steel	45hp 3cyl Triple Muir & Houston	1896 Mackie & Thomson Govan	Built as GY142 Dover for Hagerup & Doughty 1906 Transferred to Consolidated S. F. & Co. Ltd. 1923 Sold to G. Wardell, Hartlepool 1923 Registration changed to HL38 1924 Sold to Consolidated S. F. & Ice Co. Ltd. 1924 Transferred to Lowestoft 1925 Registration changed to LT93 1936 Sold for scrapping

Name/Fishing Registration At Lowestoft	Official No. Call Sign	Gross Tonnage Net Tonnage	Dimensions(ft) Construction	Propulsion Unit/Make	Build Date Build Yard Build Location	History
Eastward Ho! LT95	109058 RDVN	162 53	105 x 21 x 11 Iron	55hp 3cyl Triple Tindall	1898 Cook, Welton & Gemmell Hull	Built as H415 Eastward Ho! for S. T. White &Co. 1920 Sold to W. Barton, Whitby 1920 Registration changed to WY106 1924 Sold to Consolidated S. F. & Ice Co. ltd. 1924 Transferred to Lowestoft on 20th December 1925 Registration changed to LT95 1936 Sold to Clayton & Davies, Dunston-on-Tyne for scrapping
Erillus GY234	136997 MDMX	201 78	112 x 22 x 12 Steel	68hp 3cyl Triple Smith's Dock	1914 Smith's Dock Middlesboro.	Built for the Consolidated Steam Fishing & Ice Co. Ltd. 1914-18 War Service 1939-40 War Service 1954 Transferred to Lowestoft on 26th April 1955 Sold for scrapping to C. Dorkins, Gateshead 1955 Left Lowestoft on 21st April
Eudocia LT113	098727 MQJB	147 68	101 x 21 x 11 Iron	45hp 3cyl Triple Holmes	1891 Cook, Welton & Gemmell Hull	Built as H130 Eudocia for Hellyer S. F. Co. Ltd. 1914 Sold to T. Larder, Aberdeen 1917 Sold to H. Smethurst and others, Grimsby 1917 Registration changed to GY1049 1924 Sold to J. Mein 1924 Sold to Consolidated S. F. & Ice Co. Ltd. 1924 Transferred to Lowestoft on 6th November 1924 Registration to LT113 1941 Sold to Dinas Steam Fishing Co. Ltd. 1945 Sold to Adaform Ltd., Liverpool. 1950 Sold for scrap
Exeter GY426	108482					See below for details
Exeter LT139	108482 MKGR	165 64	104 x 21 x 11 Steel	45hp 3cyl Triple Muir & Houston	1897 Mackie & Thomson Govan	Built as GY426 Exeter for Hagerup & Doughty 1906 Transferred to Consolidated S. F. & Ice Co. Ltd. 1917-19 War service 1920 Transferred to Lowestoft on 9th October 1925 Registration changed to LT139 1929 Sold to J. Gough, Milford Haven 1939 Sold to T. S. Yolland and J. Yolland, Fleetwood 1941 Bombed and sank 5 Miles S. W. of Ballycotton. on 29th March

Name/Fishing Registration At Lowestoft	Official No. Call Sign	Gross Tonnage Net Tonnage	Dimensions(ft) Construction	Propulsion Unit/Make	Build Date Build Yard Build Location	History
Falmouth GY428	108483					See below for details
Falmouth LT143	108483 GNNJ	165 64	104 x 21 x 11 Steel	45hp 3cyl Triple Muir & Houston	1897 Mackie & Thomson Govan	Built as GY428 Falmouth for Hagerup & Doughty 1906 Transferred to Consolidated S. F. & Ice Co. Ltd. 1914-19 War Service 1915 Renamed Falmouth II 1919 Renamed Falmouth 1920 Transferred to Lowestoft on 9th October 1925 Registration changed to LT143 1938 Sold to Pair Fishing Co. Ltd., Milford Haven 1938 Registration changed to M286 1945 Sold to Standard Steam Fishing Co. Ltd. 1945 Registration changed to GY25 1945 Mined and sunk in North Sea on 12th April
Fidelia LT187	099544 MQVN	147 61	100 x 20 x 11 Iron	50hp 3cyl Triple Holmes	1891 Cook, Welton & Gemmell Hull	Built as H177 Fidelia for F. & T. Ross Ltd., Hull 1925 Sold to Consolidated S. F. & Ice Co. Ltd. 1925 Transferred to Lowestoft on 3rd January 1925 Registration changed to LT187 1941 Sunk during an air attack on 5th May in Lowestoft Harbour whilst on Admiralty service
Flavia GY1335	144364 GJJD	202 76	115 x 22 x 12 Steel	75hp 3cyl Triple Mumford	1919 Rennie, Forrestt Wivenhoe	Built as HMT William Harrison ("Strath" class) 1920 Registered as LO319 1921 Sold to Consolidated S. F. & Ice Co. Ltd. 1921 Became GY1335 Flavia 1929 Transferred to Lowestoft on 20th June 1935 Sold to John Craig and others, Aberdeen 1935 Registration changed to A373 1940 Lost on 28th August in North Sea, unknown cause
Fleetwood GY166	106688	163 63	104 x 20 x 11 Steel	45hp 3cyl Triple Muir & Houston	1896 Mackie & Thomson Govan	Built as GY166 Fleetwood for Hagerup & Doughty 1906 Transferred to Consolidated S. F. & Ice Co. Ltd. 1920 Transferred to Lowestoft on 8th October 1920 Total loss on 24th November on Scroby Sand

Name/Fishing Registration At Lowestoft	Official No. Call Sign	Gross Tonnage Net Tonnage	Dimensions (ft) Construction	Propulsion Unit/Make	Build Date Build Yard Build Location	History
Flixton LT320	144162	201 88	116 x 22 x 12 Steel	57hp 3cyl Triple Fleming Ferguson	1919 Fleming & Ferguson Paisley	Built as HMT William Harvey ("Strath" class) 1919 Completed as ME68 River Orchy 1920 Owned by Montrose Steam Fishing Co. Ltd. 1925 Sold to Consolidated S. F. & Ice Co. Ltd. 1925 Registration changed to GY291 1938 Transferred to Lowestoft on 2nd November 1938 Registration changed to LT320 1939 Renamed Flixton 1940-43 War Service 1943 Sold to R. Hastie & Sons Ltd., North Shields 1943 Registration changed to SN120 1948 Sold to Norway, renamed Wenche
Framlingham LT252	113214 MGQL	169 69	104 x 21 x 11 Iron	55hp 3cyl Triple Holmes	1900 Cochrane & Cooper Selby	Built as GY1208 Rodrigo for Sir G. F. Sleight 1938 Sold to Consolidated Fisheries Ltd. 1938 Transferred to Lowestoft on 6th December 1939 Became LT252 Framlingham 1940 Damaged by bombing, 20 miles S. E. of Fastnet 1944 Sold to C. Dobson 1944 Registration changed to GY1 1945 Sold to Elkington Estates Ltd. 1949 Sold to Respondo Trawlers Ltd., Milford Haven 1952 Sold for scrapping
Fritton LT297	146142 GSSF	203 78	115 x 22 x 12 Steel	75hp 3cyl Triple Beardmore	1918 R. Williamson Workington	Built as HMT Thomas Dear ("Strath" class) 1921 Sold to Consolidated S. F. & Ice Co. Ltd. 1921 Registered as GY1337 1922 Renamed Ninette 1930 Transferred to Lowestoft on 17th October 1938 Became LT297 Fritton 1955 Sold to J. J. King, Gateshead for scrapping 1955 Left Lowestoft on 21st April
Gardenia LT117	099190	146 70	97 x 21 x 11 Iron	45hp 3cyl Triple Holmes	1891 Cochrane, Cooper & Schofield Beverley	Built as GY402 for N. E. Steam Fishing Co. Ltd. 1919 Sold to T. W. Baskcomb 1935 Sold to Consolidated Fisheries Ltd. 1935 Transferred to Lowestoft on 11th November 1935 Registration changed to LT117 1939 Sold to C. Valkenburg, Antwerp 1939 Left Lowestoft on 3rd February

Name/Fishing Registration At Lowestoft	Official No. Call Sign	Gross Tonnage Net Tonnage	Dimensions(ft) Construction	Propulsion Unit/Make	Build Date Build Yard Build Location	History
Grimenco LT97	110878	153 60	101 x 21 x 11 Steel	40hp 3cyl Triple North East Marine	1899 Wood, Skinner Bill Quay	Built as GY9 Alroy for Ellis, Spence & Co. Ltd. 1914 Sold to J.W. Smethurst 1914 Renamed Grimenco 1919 Sold to Streonshall Fishing Co. Ltd., Whitby 1919 Registered as WY59 1924 Sold to Consolidated S. F. & Ice Co. Ltd. 1925 Transferred to Lowestoft on 13th November 1925 Registration changed to LT97 1926 Sold to France 1926 Left Lowestoft on 16th July for Dieppe
Grimsby GY168	106689	163 63	104 x 20 x 11 Steel	45hp 3cyl Triple Muir & Houston	1896 Mackie & Thomson Govan	Built for Hagerup & Doughty 1906 Transferred to Consolidated S. F. & Ice Co. Ltd. 1914-18 War Service 1921 Transferred to Lowestoft on 10th September 1922 Sold to Jas. Paton, Leith, left Lowestoft on 12th April 1922 Registration changed to LH308
Gunton LT319	143860 GJNK	202 81	116 x 22 x 12 Steel	57hp 3cyl Triple Fleming Ferguson	1917 Fleming & Ferguson Paisley	Built as HMT John Cowarder ("Strath" class) 1919 Sold to Montrose Steam Fishing Co. Ltd. 1919 Became ME86 River Nith 1923 Purchased by Consolidated S. F. & Ice Co. Ltd 1923 Registration changed to GY289 1938 Transferred to Lowestoft on 10th November 1938 Registration changed to LT319 1939 Renamed Gunton 1955 Sold to Craigwood Ltd., Aberdeen 1955 Left Lowestoft on 15th March for Aberdeen 1955 Registration changed to A12 1959 Sold for scrapping
Halifax GY442	108485					For details see below
Halifax LT144	108485 MGPR	165 63	104 x 22 x 11 Steel	45hp 3cyl Triple Muir & Houston	1897 Mackie & Thomson Govan	Built as GY442 for Hagerup & Doughty 1906 Transferred to Consolidated S. F. & Ice Co. Ltd. 1914-18 War Service 1921 Transferred to Lowestoft on 8tht September 1925 Registration changed to LT144 1940 Lost due to mine damage on 11th March off Aldeburgh

Name/Fishing Registration At Lowestoft	Official No. Call Sign	Gross Tonnage Net Tonnage	Dimensions(ft) Construction	Propulsion Unit/Make	Build Date Build Yard Build Location	History
Hopton LT317	144164 GSSG	202 88	115 x 22 x 12 Steel	75hp 3cyl Triple Beardmore	1920 Montrose SB Montrose	Built as HMT James Carrick ("Strath" class) 1920 Sold to Montrose Steam Fishing Co. Ltd. 1920 Completed as ME132 River Findhorn 1922 Sold to Consolidated S. F. & Ice Co. Ltd. 1922 Registration changed to GY276 1938 Transferred to Lowestoft on 8th September 1938 Registration changed to LT317 1939 Renamed Hopton 1941 Lost off Iceland on 8th April
Ilfracombe GY450	108486					See below for details
Ilfracombe LT148	108486 MGPS	165 63	104 x 21 x 11 Steel	45hp 3cyl Triple Muir & Houston	1897 Mackie & Thomson Govan	Built as GY450 for Hagerup & Doughty 1906 Transferred to Consolidated S. F. & Ice Co. Ltd. 1914-18 War Service 1920 Transferred to Lowestoft on 13th October 1925 Registration changed to LT148 1937 Sold to Don Trawling Co. (Milford Haven) Ltd. 1945 Sold to Cranbrook Shipping Co. Ltd. 1945 Total Loss after grounding off Ireland on 22nd September. Later refloated and broken up
Ipswich GY178	106692					See below for details
Ipswich LT128	106692 MFTZ	162 63	104 x 20 x 11 Steel	45hp 3cyl Triple Muir & Houston	1896 Mackie & Thomson Govan	Built as GY178 Ipswich for Hagerup & Doughty 1906 Transferred to Consolidated S. F. & Ice Co. Ltd. 1914-18 War Service 1920 Transferred to Lowestoft on 4th October 1925 Registration changed to LT128 1941 Sold to Boston Deep Sea Fishing Co. Ltd. 1944 Sold to Ocean Steam Trawling Co. Ltd. 1944 Registration changed to H56 1950 In the ownership of Cranbrook Shipping Ltd. 1953 Sold for scrapping at Grays, Essex

Name/Fishing Registration At Lowestoft	Official No. Call Sign	Gross Tonnage Net Tonnage	Dimensions(ft) Construction	Propulsion Unit/Make	Build Date Build Yard Build Location	History
Jonquil LT94	099187 MJVR	143 54	96 x 20 x 11 Iron	45hp 3cyl Triple Grey	1891 A. Robertson Canning Town	Built as GY391 Lynbrook for International S. F. Co. Ltd. 1898 Sold to North Eastern Steam Fishing Co. Ltd. 1902 Renamed Jonquil 1919 Sold to T. W. Baskcomb 1935 Sold to Consolidated Fisheries Ltd.. 1935 Transferred to Lowestoft on 17th November 1935 Registration changed to LT94 1953 Sold to T. W. Ward & Co. Ltd., Grays, for scrapping 1953 Left Lowestoft on 11th May
King Arthur GY11	110880					See LT157 King Charles for details
King Arthur LT157	110880					See LT157 King Charles for details
King Athelstan LT160	110884 GQLL	159 66	106 x 21 x 11 Steel	40hp 3cyl Triple Muir & Houston	1899 Schofield, Hagerup & Doughty Grimsby	Built as GY97 King Egbert for Monarch S. F. Co. 1906 Transferred to Consolidated S. F. & Ice Co. Ltd. 1915-1920 War service 1923 Transferred to Lowestoft on 26th February 1925 Registration changed to LT160 1927 Renamed King Athelstan 1953 Sold to T. W. Ward & Co. Ltd., Grays, for scrapping 1953 Left Lowestoft on 22nd April
King Canute GY1124	110923 SHFR	210 98	117 x 21 x 11 Steel	40hp 3cyl Triple Muir & Houston	1899 Schofield, Hagerup & Doughty Grimsby	Built for Monarch Steam Fishing Co. Ltd. 1906 Transferred to Consolidated S. F. & Ice Co. Ltd. 1920 Sold to W. Smith 1920 Transferred to Canute Steam Fishing Co. Ltd. 1922 Transferred to Lowestoft 1926 Port of registration changed to " Lowestoft" 1926 In use as a collier 1927 Transferred to Consolidated S. F. & Ice Co. 1927 Transferred to Grimsby

Name/Fishing Registration At Lowestoft	Official No. Call Sign	Gross Tonnage Net Tonnage	Dimensions(ft) Construction	Propulsion Unit/Make	Build Date Build Yard Build Location	History
King Charles LT157	110880 MDJJ	159 70	106 x 21 x 11 Steel	40hp 3cyl Triple Muir & Houston	1899 Schofield, Hagerup & Doughty Grimsby	Built as GY11 King Arthur for Monarch S. F. Co. 1906 Transferred to Consolidated S. F. & Ice Co. 1915-1920 War Service 1922 Transferred to Lowestoft on 27th February 1925 Registration changed to LT157 1927 Renamed King Charles 1941 Sold to Boston Deep Sea Fishing & Ice Co. Ltd. 1943 Sold to Ocean Steam Trawling Co. Ltd., Hull 1944 Sold to Partnership (Hull) Ltd., Hull 1946 Sold to Mostyn & Willey Ltd. 1947 Sold to Alan Percival, Blackpool 1948 Sold to Partnership (Hull) Ltd., Hull 1950 Sold for scrapping in Belgium
King Edward GY1195	113201					See below for details
King Edward LT169	113201 GQDX	163 73	106 x 21 x 11 Steel	40hp 3cyl Triple Muir & Houston	1900 Schofield, Hagerup & Doughty Grimsby	Built as GY1195 for Monarch S. F. Co. Ltd. 1906 Transferred to Consolidated S. F. & Ice Co. Ltd. 1915-19 War Service 1923 Transferred to Lowestoft on 24th September 1925 Registration changed to LT169 1953 Sold to T. W. Ward & Co. Ltd., Grays, for scrapping 1953 Left Lowestoft on 22nd April
King Egbert GY97	110884					See LT160 King Athelstan for details
King Egbert LT160	110884					See LT160 King Athelstan for details
King Henry GY1169	113175					See below for details
King Henry LT355	113175 MGPT	162 72	106 x 21 x 11 Steel	45hp 3cyl Triple Muir & Houston	1900 Schofield, Hagerup & Doughty Grimsby	Built as GY1169 for the Monarch S. F. Co. Ltd. 1906 Transferred to Consolidated S. F. & Ice Co. 1918-19 War Service 1925 Transferred to Lowestoft on 23rd February 1927 Registration changed to LT355 1941 Sank in Lowestoft Harbour on 13th June due to enemy action whilst on Admiralty service

Name/Fishing Registration At Lowestoft	Official No. Call Sign	Gross Tonnage Net Tonnage	Dimensions(ft) Construction	Propulsion Unit/Make	Build Date Build Yard Build Location	History
King Richard GY1181	113186					See below for details
King Richard LT161	113186 GMTW	162 74	105 x 21 x 11 Steel	45hp 3cyl Triple Muir & Houston	1900 Schofield, Hagerup & Doughty Grimsby	Built as GY1181 for Monarch S. F. Co. Ltd. 1906 Transferred to Consolidated S. F. & Ice Co. Ltd. 1915-20 War Service 1924 Transferred to Lowestoft during February 1925 Registration changed to LT161 1953 Sold for scrap to C. W. Dorking & Co. Ltd 1953 Left Lowestoft on 27th April
Kingston GY206	108442	161 63	104 x 20 x 11 Steel	45hp 3cyl Triple Muir & Houston	1897 Mackie & Thomson Govan	Built for Hagerup & Doughty 1906 Transferred to Consolidated S. F. & Ice Co. Ltd. 1915-19 War Service 1921 Transferred to Lowestoft on 2nd October 1922 Sold to Mason Trawlers Ltd., Fleetwood 1922 Left Lowestoft for Fleetwood on 29th April 1926 Registration changed to FD144
Kuvera GY381	140790 GRGS	202 87	115 x 22 x 12 Steel	74hp 3cyl Plenty	1919 Ouse SB Hook	Built as HMT John Heath ("Strath" class) 1919 In the ownership of F. Pearce, Cleethorpes 1922 Owned by Consolidated S. F. as GY381 Kuvera 1929 Transferred to Lowestoft on 7th January 1933 Transferred to Grimsby on 19th January 1935 Sold to R. Baxter, Aberdeen 1935 Registration changed to A384 1945 Sold to Granton 1949 In the ownership of Planet Fishing Co., Ltd. 1950 Total Loss on 26th January in North Sea

Name/Fishing Registration At Lowestoft	Official No. Call Sign	Gross Tonnage Net Tonnage	Dimensions(ft) Construction	Propulsion Unit/Make	Build Date Build Yard Build Location	History
Lavenham LT274	113232 MGWR	166 65	101 x 21 x 11 Iron	55hp 3cyl Triple Holmes	1902 Cook, Welton & Gemmell Beverley	Built as GY1232 Rosco for Sir G. F. Sleight 1938 Sold to Consolidated Fisheries Ltd. 1938 Transferred to Lowestoft on 29th November 1938 Became LT274 Lavenham 1939 Transferred to Grimsby on 8th October 1943 Sold to Elkington Estates Ltd. 1944 Registration changed to GY3 1947 Sold to Yolland Bros., Milford Haven 1950 In the ownership of Repondo Trawlers Ltd. 1952 Sold for Scrapping
Leeds GY207	108443					See below for details
Leeds LT131	108443 MGRV	162 63	104 x 20 x 11 Steel	45hp 3cyl Triple Muir & Houston	1897 Mackie & Thomson Govan	Built as GY207 for Hagerup & Doughty 1906 Transferred to Consolidated S. F. & Ice Co. 1924 Transferred to Lowestoft on 22nd September 1925 Registration changed to LT131 1941 Sold to Boston Deep Sea Fishing Co. Ltd. 1944 Sold to S. Uglow 1947 Sold to Respondo Trawlers Ltd., Milford Haven 1951 Sold for scrapping
Loddon LT309	141916 GPJF	199 87	115 x 22 x 12 Steel	75hp 3cyl Triple Allen	1919 Scott & Son Bowling	Built as HMT George Lane ("Strath" class) 1919 Sold to Montrose Steam Fishing Co. Ltd 1919 Completed as ME46 River Kelvin 1922 Sold to Consolidated S. T. & Ice Co. Ltd. 1922 Registration changed to GY272 1938 Transferred to Lowestoft on 6th September 1938 Registered as LT309 1939 Renamed Loddon 1955 Sold to Craigwood Ltd., Aberdeen 1955 Left Lowestoft on 15th March 1955 Registered as A8 1958 Sold to Wood & Davidson Ltd. 1960 Sold to British Iron & Steel Corp. for scrapping

Name/Fishing Registration At Lowestoft	Official No. Call Sign	Gross Tonnage Net Tonnage	Dimensions(ft) Construction	Propulsion Unit/Make	Build Date Build Yard Build Location	History
Newhaven LT134	108449 MGPX	161 63	104 x 20 x 11 Steel	45hp 3cyl Triple Muir & Houston	1897 Mackie & Thomson Govan	Built as GY232 for Hagerup & Doughty 1906 Transferred to Consolidated S. F. & Ice Co. 1918-1919 War Service 1920 Transferred to Lowestoft on 16th October 1925 Registration changed to LT134 1940 Sunk by mine on 15th January, 18 miles SSE of Lowestoft
Ninette GY1337	146142					Refer to LT297 Fritton for history
Oldham GY538	109513	165 52	104 x 22 x 11 Steel	45hp 3cyl Triple Muir & Houston	1896 Mackie & Thomson Govan	Built for Hagerup & Doughty 1906 Transferred to Consolidated S. F. & Ice Co. 1920 Transferred to Lowestoft on 2nd October 1922 Sold to F. Bullard, Aberdeen 1922 Left Lowestoft on 12th June 1922 Registration changed to A904 1931 Sold to D. Pettit, registration changed to M153
Ostrich LT107	096246 MFWQ	146 69	97 x 21 x 11 Steel	45hp 3cyl Triple Holmes	1891 Cochrane, Cooper & Schofield Beverley	Built as GY311 for T. Baskcomb 1903 Sold to H. L. Taylor 1922 Sold to R. D. Clarke 1924 Sold to Consolidated S. T. & Ice Co. Ltd. 1924 Transferred to Lowestoft in 11th December 1924 Registration changed to LT107 1953 Sold to J. J. King, Gateshead for scrapping 1953 Left Lowestoft on 30th April towed by Adrian
Rendlesham LT265	113233 MGQP	166 64	101 x 21 x 11 Iron	55hp 3cyl Triple Holmes	1902 Cook, Welton & Gemmell Beverley	Built as GY1233 Rosareno for Sir G. F. Sleight & others 1933 Transferred to Sleight and Humphreys 1938 Sold to Consolidated Fisheries Ltd. 1938 Transferred to Lowestoft on 5th December 1938 Became LT265 Rendlesham 1940 Total loss on 5th December after hitting submerged rocks off Cape Clear.

Name/Fishing Registration At Lowestoft	Official No. Call Sign	Gross Tonnage Net Tonnage	Dimensions(ft) Construction	Propulsion Unit/Make	Build Date Build Yard Build Location	History
Rochester GY671	109529					See below for details
Rochester LT153	109529	165 64	104 x 22 x 11 Steel	45hp 3cyl Triple Muir & Houston	1898 Mackie & Thomson Govan	Built as GY671 for Hagerup and Doughty 1906 Transferred to Consolidated S. F. & Ice Co. Ltd. 1914-19 War Service 1920 Transferred to Lowestoft on 21st October 1925 Registration changed to LT153 1941 Sold to Boston Deep Sea Fishing Co. Ltd. 1944 Sold to Ocean Steam Trawling Co. Ltd. 1944 Sank with mine damage on 27th July in the North Sea
Richmond GY255	108455					See below for details
Richmond LT135	108455 MGPY	161 63	104 x 20 x 11 Steel	45hp 3cyl Triple Muir & Houston	1897 Mackie & Thomson Govan	Built as GY255 for Hagerup & Doughty 1906 Transferred to Consolidated S. F. & Ice Co. 1918-19 War service 1921 Transferred to Lowestoft on 24th March 1925 Registration changed to LT135 1927 Sold to John MacLeod, Liverpool 1935 Sold to Waterloo Steam Trawling Co. Ltd. 1935 Sold to George Singleton, Milford 1935 Scrapped
Sabina GY1329	144286 GZNJ	202 77	115 x 22 x 12 Steel	75hp 3cyl Triple Mumford	1919 Rennie, Forrestt Wivenhoe	Built as HMT Charles Doyle ("Strath" class) 1921 Sold to Consolidated S. F. & Ice Co. Ltd 1922 Became GY1329 Sabina 1930 Transferred to Lowestoft on 21st October 1933 Transferred to Grimsby on 3rd January 1935 Sold to John Craig and others, Aberdeen 1935 Registration changed to A363 1940-45 War Service 1947 Sold to J. W. Tomlinson, and others, N.Shields 1960 Sold for scrapping

Name/Fishing Registration At Lowestoft	Official No. Call Sign	Gross Tonnage Net Tonnage	Dimensions(ft) Construction	Propulsion Unit/Make	Build Date Build Yard Build Location	History
Saxmundham LT286	118931 GFNZ	170 64	105 x 21 x 11 Steel	55hp 3cyl Triple Holmes	1904 Cook, Welton & Gemmell Beverley	Built as GY22 Roto for Sir G. F. Sleight and others 1915-20 War Service 1933 Transferred to Sleight and Humphreys 1938 Sold to Consolidated Fisheries Ltd. 1938 Transferred to Lowestoft on 1st December 1939 Became LT286 Saxmundham 1945 Sold to the Raw Materials Supply Corp. Ltd. 1950 Sold to Cranbrook Shipping Co. Ltd. 1952 Sold for scrapping on Tyneside
Scarborough GY266	108456					See below for details
Scarborough LT136	108456 GFFV	161 63	104 x 20 x 11 Steel	45hp 3cyl Triple Muir & Thomson	1897 Mackie & Thomson Govan	Built as GY266 for Hagerup & Doughty 1906 Transferred to Consolidated S. F. & Ice Co. Ltd. 1920 Transferred to Lowestoft on 5th October 1925 Registration changed to LT136 1937 Sold to Don Trawling Co. Ltd. 1945 Sold to Cranbrook Shipping Co. Ltd. 1952 Sold for scrapping on Tyneside
Shamrock LT406	110758 MDDK	184 65	110 x 21 x 11 Iron	50hp 3cyl Triple Holmes	1899 Cook, Welton & Gemmell Hull	Built as H483 1907 In the ownership of J. Duncan, Liverpool 1928 Sold to Consolidated Fisheries Ltd. 1928 Transferred to Lowestoft on 8th October 1928 Registration changed to LT406 1945 Acquired by M.O.W.T., fishing registry closed 1947 Towed away from Lowestoft by tug Scotsman
Thistle LT408	114511	158 61	105 x 20 x 11 Steel	50hp 3cyl Triple Shields	1901 J. Eltringham S. Shields	Built as SN311 for Purdy S. F. Co. Ltd. 1920 Sold and registration changed to A300 1928 Sold to Consolidated Fisheries Ltd. 1928 Transferred to Lowestoft on 1st November 1928 Registration changed to LT408 1936 Sold for scrapping to Clayton & Davies 1936 Left Lowestoft for the Tyne on 26th April

Name/Fishing Registration At Lowestoft	Official No. Call Sign	Gross Tonnage Net Tonnage	Dimensions(ft) Construction	Propulsion Unit/Make	Build Date Build Yard Build Location	History
Valentia GY568	109518					See below for details
Valentia LT150	109518	164 64	104 x 21 x 11 Steel	45hp 3cyl Triple Muir & Houston	1898 Irvine SBE Irvine	Built as GY568 by Hagerup & Doughty 1906 Transferred to Consolidated S. F. & Ice Co. 1920 Transferred to Lowestoft on 14th October 1925 Registration changed to LT150 1938 Sold to Pair Fishing Co. Ltd., Milford Haven 1938 Registration changed to M267 1945 Sold to Standard Steam Fishing Co. Ltd. 1946 Sold to Valentia Fishing Co. Ltd. 1946 Registration changed to GY26 1949 Sold for scrapping
Valeria GY818	109813					See below for details
Valeria LT156	109813 MGQB	189 76	113 x 21 x 11 Iron	55hp 3cyl Triple Holmes	1898 Cochrane & Cooper Beverley	Built as GY818 for Arctic Steam Fishing Co. Ltd. 1916 Sold to Consolidated S. F. & Ice Co. Ltd. 1917-18 War Service 1924 Transferred to Lowestoft on 1st April 1925 Registration changed to LT156 1940 Bombed and sunk near The Smalls on 18th August
Volta LT180	098706	157 60	101 x 21 x 11 Iron	45hp 3cyl Triple Holmes	1890 Cochrane & Cooper Beverley	Built as H111 for F. & T. Ross Ltd. 1923 Sold to Consolidated S. F. & Ice Co. Ltd. 1925 Transferred to Lowestoft on 7th January 1925 Registration changed to LT180 1938 Sold to C. Valkenburg, Antwerp 1938 Left Lowestoft on 14th October for Belgium
Walsingham LT279	118933	170 64	105 x 21 x 11 Steel	55hp 3cyl Triple Holmes	1904 Cook, Welton & Gemmell Beverley	Built as GY23 Renovo for Sir G. F. Sleight 1917-19 War Service 1933 Transferred to Sleight and Humphreys 1938 Sold to Consolidated Fisheries Ltd. 1938 Transferred to Lowestoft 1938 Registration changed to LT279 1939 Transferred to Grimsby on 8th October 1941 Total loss after a collision in the English Channel

Name/Fishing Registration At Lowestoft	Official No. Call Sign	Gross Tonnage Net Tonnage	Dimensions(ft) Construction	Propulsion Unit/Make	Build Date Build Yard Build Location	History
Whitby GY524	108499 MGQC	164 64	104 x 21 x 11 Steel	45hp 3cyl Triple Muir & Houston	1898 Irvine SBE Irvine	Built for Hagerup & Doughty 1906 Transferred to Consolidated S. F. & Ice Co. Ltd. 1918-19 War Service 1920 Transferred to Lowestoft on 7th October 1922 Sold to Fleetwood owner 1922 Left Lowestoft for Fleetwood on 10th May 1922 Sold to T. W. Mason & T. Cardwell 1926 Registration changed to FD147 1930 Sold to Pettit & Youds, Milford Haven 1931 Registration changed to M141 1936 In the ownership of F. Youds, Milford Haven 1938 Sold to J. C. Llewellyn, Milford Haven 1941 Total loss after an air attack and bombing in the North Sea on 4th April.
Wistaria LT97	096242 MJVW	143 53	96 x 20 x 11 Iron	44hp 3cyl Triple Grey	1891 A. Robinson London	Built as GY302 Lynton for International S. F. Co. Ltd. 1898 Sold to North Eastern S. F Co. Ltd. 1903 Renamed Wistaria 1914-1919 War Service 1916 Renamed Wistaria II 1919 Sold to T. W. Baskcomb 1919 Renamed Wistaria 1935 Sold to Consolidated Fisheries Ltd. 1935 Transferred to Lowestoft on 12th November 1935 Registration changed to LT97 1939 Sold to C. Valkenburg, Antwerp 1939 Left Lowestoft on 7th February
Witham GY283	128772 GLTW	205 93	115 x 22 x 12 Steel	90hp 3cyl Triple Abdela & Mitchell	1919 Abdela & Mitchell Queensferry	Built as HMT Stephen Kenny ("Strath " class) 1919 Completed as BN20 Witham 1923 Purchased by Consolidated S. F. & Ice Co. Ltd 1923 Registration changed to GY283 1939 Transferred to Lowestoft on 19th July 1955 Sold to T. W. Ward & Co. Grays for scrapping 1955 Left Lowestoft on 5th April

Name/Fishing Registration At Lowestoft	Official No. Call Sign	Gross Tonnage Net Tonnage	Dimensions(ft) Construction	Propulsion Unit/Make	Build Date Build Yard Build Location	History
Wolseley LT410	114529	159 61	105 x 21 x 11 Steel	55hp 3cyl Triple Shields	1903 J. Eltringham S. Shields	Built as SN345 for Warrior Steam Fishing Co. Ltd. 1917 Sold to H. C. Baker, Grimsby 1917 Registration changed to GY1067 1917 Sold to W. Hill 1918 Sold to Northern Steam Fishing Co. Ltd. 1920 Sold to A. Walker, Aberdeen 1920 Registration changed to A393 1928 Sold to Consolidated S. F. & Ice Co. Ltd. 1928 Transferred to Lowestoft on 27th October 1928 Registration changed to LT410 1944 Sold to R. M. Brackenbury and others, Grimsby 1945 Registration changed to GY23 1945 Sold to Gt. Grimsby & East Coast S. F. Co. Ltd. 1946 Sold to Danebury Fishing Co. Ltd 1949 Sold to Holland for scrapping
Xania GY330	108470					See below for details
Xania LT138	108470 GFFS	161 63	104 x 20 x 11 Steel	45hp 3cyl Triple Muir & Houston	1897 Mackie & Thomson Govan	Built as GY330 for Hagerup & Doughty 1906 Transferred to Consolidated S. F. & Ice Co. 1914-1919 War service 1921 Transferred to Lowestoft on 7th October 1925 Registration changed to LT138 1937 Sold to Pair Fishing Co. Ltd., Milford Haven 1940 Total loss on 16th March after collision with LT123 Aberdeen
Yulan LT96	099165 MSVT	144 54	96 x 20 x 11 Iron	45hp 3cyl Triple Amos & Smith	1891 A. Robertson Canning Town	Built as GY348 Lynmouth for International S. F. Co. 1891 Completed for G. Doughty 1898 Sold to North Eastern S. F. Co. Ltd. 1904 Renamed Yulan 1919 Sold to T. W. Baskcomb 1935 Sold to Consolidated Fisheries Ltd. 1935 Transferred to Lowestoft on 24th November 1935 Registration changed to LT96 1945 Sold to Wendover Fishing Co. (Grimsby) Ltd. 1946 Sold to Dorida S. T. Co. Ltd. 1946 Registration changed to GY64 1948 Sold to Seago & Co., Yarmouth, for scrapping

Name/Fishing Registration At Lowestoft	Official No. Call Sign	Gross Tonnage Net Tonnage	Dimensions(ft) Construction	Propulsion Unit/Make	Build Date Build Yard Build Location	History
Zetland GY760	109549					See below for details
Zetland LT154	109549	165 64	104 x 21 x 11 Steel	45hp 3cyl Triple Muir & Houston	1898 Mackie & Thomson Govan	Built as GY760 Zetland for Hagerup & Doughty 1906 Transferred to Consolidated S. F. & Ice Co. 1917-19 War service 1924 Transferred to Lowestoft 1925 Registration changed to LT154 1936 Sold for scrapping to Clayton & Davies 1936 Left Lowestoft for the Tyne on 26th April
Zodiac LT173	096235	149 75	100 x 20 x 11 Iron	45hp 3cyl Triple Muir & Houston	1891 Mackie & Thomson Govan	Built as GY286 Zodiac for Grimsby & North Sea S. T. Co. 1900 Sold to Norway 1906 Sold to Grimsby & North Sea Steam T. Co. Ltd. 1906 Registration changed to GY151 1908 Sold to S. Green & D. James, St. Dogmaels, Cardigan 1917 Sold to W. Would 1920 Sold to Woodbury S. F. Co. Ltd. 1925 Sold to Consolidated Steam Fishing & Ice Co. Ltd. 1925 Transferred to Lowestoft on 17th January 1925 Registration changed to LT173 1933 Sold for scrapping
Zonia LT118	109525	150 58	100 x 20 x 11 Steel	41hp 3cyl Triple Ross & Duncan	1898 Mackie & Thomson Govan	Built as GY605 Apollo for Orient S. F. Co. Ltd. 1904 Sold to Norway 1914 Sold to Orient S. F. Co. Ltd., Grimsby 1914 Became GY227 Zonia 1914-1919 War Service 1920 Sold to Direct Fish Supplies Ltd. 1920 Registration changed to DO88 1929 Sold to T. W. Baskcomb 1929 Registration changed to GY139 1935 Sold to Consolidated Fisheries Ltd. 1936 Transferred to Lowestoft on 10th January 1936 Registration changed to LT118 1941 Sold to Cranley Shipping Co. Ltd., London 1950 Sold for scrapping

OTHER VESSELS

Diesel Trawler

Name/Fishing Registration At Lowestoft	Official No. Call Sign	Gross Tonnage Net Tonnage	Dimensions(ft) Construction	Propulsion Unit/Make	Build Date Build Yard Build Location	History
Vanessa Ann LT254	183981 GNPF	168 55	103 x 22 x 11 Steel	540hp 6cyl Diesel British Polar	1951 Richards Lowestoft	Built for Consolidated Fisheries Ltd. (Yard No. 403) 1955 Transferred to Rhondda Fishing Co. Ltd. 1957 Sold to Dalby Steam Fishing Co. Ltd. 1958 Registration changed to FD133 1971 Sold to Putford Enterprises Ltd. 1971 Converted for use as a offshore standby vessel 1972 Transferred to Keithly Enterprises Ltd. 1973 Transferred to F. E. Catchpole and re-engined 1982 Sold to Clipper Promotions Inc. for conversion to a topsail schooner. Registered in Fleetwood.

Vanessa Ann in Fleetwood ownership

After conversion, *Vanessa Ann* at Great Yarmouth

OTHER VESSELS

Coasters/Colliers

Name/Fishing Registration At Lowestoft	Official No. Call Sign	Gross Tonnage Net Tonnage	Dimensions(ft) Construction	Propulsion Unit/Make	Build Date Build Yard Build Location	History
East Anglian Lowestoft	140511 MGRW	870 419	198 x 31 x 12 Steel	97hp 3cyl Triple McColl & Pollock	1917 W. Harkess Middlesboro.	Built as Suffolk Coast for Coast Lines Ltd. 1938 Sold to Kyle Shipping Co. Ltd. 1938 Renamed Kylebank 1939 Sold to Consolidated Fisheries Ltd. for £7250 1939 Renamed East Anglian 1939 Registered at Lowestoft 1946 Sold to Grace & Chancellor Ltd. 1946 Renamed Sussex Oak 1954 Sold for scrapping
George Frusher Lowestoft	113975 MFJJ	662 447	189 x 29 x 10 Steel	89hp 2cyl Compound Lidgewood	1901 J. Fullerton Paisley	Built as Carlston 1901 In the ownership of Glasgow Steam Coasters Ltd. 1916 Sold to E. Johnson & Co. Ltd. 1926 Sold to J. Kelly Ltd., Belfast 1927 Sold to Consolidated S. F & Ice Co. Ltd. 1927 Registered at Lowestoft 1927 Renamed George Frusher 1938 Sold for scrapping in Belgium
Mons Lowestoft	139635 MBQL	641 359	178 x 29 x 11 Steel	77hp 3cyl Triple Pern	1919 Dible Southampton	Built as Southminster (of Cardiff) 1929 Sold to Consolidated Fisheries Ltd. 1929 Became Mons and registered at Grimsby 1938 Sold to Belgian owners 1939 Sold to Consolidated Fisheries Ltd. 1939 Registered at Lowestoft 1940 Sold to Chas. Strubin & Co., London 1942 Sold to Derwent Steam Shipping Co. Ltd. 1942 Registered at Newcastle

The crew of a Lowestoft steam trawler hauling on a fine day in the North Sea

At Sea with Consolidated

In the 1930's, a much respected nautical magazine featured an article on a fishing trip on a Consolidated steam trawler. Today, it gives an impression of life aboard a steam trawler approximately 70 years ago. The following is based on that article.

Note

Some of the expressions and terms used in this 1930's article differ somewhat from those in the 21st Century.

On board a Consolidated Steam Trawler

Our home for this fishing trip is a steam powered coal fired vessel of just over 100 feet. She is high in the bows and low in the stern, not what one would call handsome. Neither is she as spruce as a yacht. Fishing is a messy business. Once at sea, there is no time for anything but catching, cleaning and stowing fish, with brief intervals for meals and almost equally brief intervals for sleep. Ten men including our supernumerary self join the ship in the dock. Besides the skipper and mate, there are two engineers, a trimmer a bos'n, two deckies, that is deckhands, and a cook. Some of the crew including the skipper, mate and the engineers sleep aft, the rest of the men have quarters forrard. There, too, are the ice, rope and net stores. The foredeck, made of steel and rusty

Off the Dogger Bank on a steam trawler

like almost everything else, is more or less clear except for the hatch giving access to the fish-hold. Almost amidships is the steam-winch, a huge affair, the drums of which can accommodate hundreds of feet of steel wire, the warp for towing the trawl. Abaft the winch is the wheel-house dominating the whole ship. Beneath this is the galley. Next come the engine room and boiler casing, and finally the cabin skylight followed by the dinghy. We have two masts, the mizzen in the stern carrying a very sooty sail, useful for keeping the ship's head to wind. We have a salt encrusted funnel, much higher than would seem necessary, and are very fortunate in having a wireless set and an electric installation in part of the ship, with paraffin in other parts for lighting. Some of the trawlers have acetylene lights. There is talk of the ship being fitted with a lavatory hut, with a seat and a tub underneath, this would be much better than using the barrel and bucket out in the open, as we do now. You can read our registration number painted conspicuously on the vessel, at some considerable distance, although there is rust now in place of some of the numbers. She is fitted with gallows both port and starboard, and carries two sets of gear.

We have now been at sea for sometime. We no longer think our end is near when the trawler rolls scuppers under, as is her playful way. We are getting used to the unaccommodating texture of oilskins. We are learning to breathe in the stuffy, overcrowded, overheated cabin and to sleep above the thudding and racing screw within sound of clanging shovels and cleaning bars. The food no longer appears to us unappetising. In fact, we now enjoy it. To-night the skipper says, we shall have our gear down for the first time. At noon today there were trawlers in sight on all sides, all apparently heading like us, for the fishing grounds. Then a blanket of fog enfolded us and sirens moaned in many keys. At this time of year, night falls early, but we still bucketed forward in the gloom through a nasty cross sea.

From time to time, the skipper ordered a cast of the lead. The soundings told him where we were, and he groped his way through the fog with, as it were, his hand on the sea-floor.

At midnight a slant of wind disperses the fog and we find ourselves in the midst of several trawlers lit up like a town.

All hands are called. "Port Side!" orders the skipper. The great "otter boards", shod with iron and tremendously heavy, are unlashed. It is they which, like under-water kites, will keep the mouth of the net open. The warp is led through its appropriate pulleys, the net spread clear of obstructions. A turn of the wheel brings the ship's head in the right direction. "Let go!" yells the skipper, and five tons of complicated gear disappear from sight into the water.

The light from the big electric lamps under reflecting shades floods the deck and a watery circle round us. The warp is paid out till the trawl lies on the sea-bottom. Slowly the vessel takes the strain. The trawl "bites," the warp tautens and we move steadily forward along the appointed track. The vessel must have sufficient way on her to keep the net open, and tows the gear along the seabed for three to four hours.

The order is given for the "pounds" to be got ready. Stout boards, slipped into upright sockets, divide the foredeck into compartments two feet or so deep. Baskets are dragged from some obscure hiding place. Ice is chipped into fragments. Mysterious board constructions are being erected in the recesses of the hold.

There is a bitter north-easterly blowing, spray freezes and sheathes the bulwarks and rigging with a coating of ice.

Three hours or so after shooting the trawl, the word is given to haul. The winch rattles, bucks, leaks steam and then begins to roar into action. Slowly, steadily the warps come inboard, festooned with clinging weed. The ship lists to port. The skipper looks almost pleased; the greater the list the heavier the catch, or we could have some big stones! The warps now hang up and down; the trawl has left the bottom. Finally, the otter boards come gleaming into view and are lashed in place. Next, we see the foot and head-ropes, then the belly of the trawl, strangely agitated on the surface of the sea. Engineers, stoker, cook, all come to give a hand. The great net is gripped by half frozen fingers and secured.

Four members of the crew mending the nets at night

A rope is passed round the net above the mass of fish in the cod-end, and, by means of a tackle rigged on the foremast, the whole net is hoisted bodily on board.
The cod-end, gleaming white with half a ton or so of fish, hangs over the pounds. The mate seizes the cod-rope tugs and leaps aside just in time to avoid being buried by the cascade of fish that tumbles into the receptacles prepared for it.

Sorting the Catch

There is a rapid inspection of the net. No, not a mesh is broken, which is good fortune since hundreds are frequently torn. Overside with it again, then! Before it has reached the bottom and the ship has started to move on her course, the crew, up to the knees in slimy, slippery fish, get to work. The whole catch must be sorted and cleaned and stowed away before the next haul is made. Immature fish, inedible fish, masses of weed, starfish by the hundred, all are jerked overside to the screaming gulls. Then the job of cleaning begins. As fast as the fish is cleaned, it is thrown into the hold to be stacked neatly there - a layer of fish, then a layer of ice, then a layer of fish and so on. "All clear!" A hose is rigged and the deck pounds swilled out. Cookie distributes mugs of tea. There is just time to scald one's throat with this before the trawl is hauled again.
Trawling is a continuous process of shooting and hauling. Night and day, day in and day out, every three or four hours, a fresh haul is made until, with her hold full and just enough coal left in her bunkers to get her home, the trawler leaves astern the fishing grounds and makes for port. The exhausted crew are trying to catch up arrears of sleeps, nursing wounds and salt water boils, and planning how to spend their pay, planning too perhaps, menus on which fish does not figure!
At last, we can wash and take off our working clothes!
Once in port the trawler's catch is landed. After a stay of two days or so for bunkers, victualling and any repairs, she is again heading out for the fishing grounds to repeat the same routine.

A TYPICAL LOWESTOFT SUNRISE ON 23RD AUGUST 1924 WITH THE *DERBY* HEADING FOR THE FISHING GROUNDS.

SELECT BIBLIOGRAPHY

Down The Harbour 1955-1995 by Malcolm White (White-1998)
40 years of fishing vessels, owners, the harbour and shipyards at Lowestoft

Fishing with Diversity by Malcolm White (White-2000)
A Portrait of the Colne Group of Lowestoft

A Century of Fishing by Malcolm White (White-1999)
Fishing from Great Yarmouth and Lowestoft 1899-1999

Consolidated Fisheries Ltd. (Various)
Company Logs, Diaries, Landing Books and Ledgers

Consolidated Steam Fishing & Ice Co., (Grimsby), Ltd. (Various)
Company Logs, Diaries, Landing Books and Ledgers

Fishing News Various Editions (EMAP)
Olsen's Fisherman's Nautical Almanack Various (Dennis)
Lowestoft Journal Various Editions (NNC)
Maritime Directories Various Editions (HMSO)
PLRS Newsletters and Documents Various (PLRS)
Introduction to Trawling by A. Hodson (Hodson)
Lloyds Register of Shipping Various Editions (Lloyds)
Mercantile Navy List Various Editions (HMSO)
The Steam Trawlers and Liners of Grimsby by C. B. Cox (Cox-1988)

PHOTOGRAPHIC INDEX

SUBJECT	PAGE
Aberdeen	18
Ampere	27, 36
Bellerophon	Back Cover
Bellona	Front Cover
Belton	40
Boreas	35
Bucentaur	15, 35
City of Aberdeen	Back Cover
Croton	28
Crownies Laid Up	15
Dahlia	28
Derby	71
Dereham	38
Eastward Ho!	23
Erillus	41
Falmouth	25
Flavia	34
Fleetwood	26
Framlingham	21
Franc-Tireur	36
Fritton	31,40
George Frusher	27
Gunton	5, 42
Ipswich	20
King Athelstan	16
King Canute	17
King Charles	6, 22
King Edward	19, 41
King Henry	24, 30
King Richard	1
Kuvera	34
Kylebank	39
Lavenham	31
Leeds	25
Loddon	31, 42
Mons	19
Naval Trawler	30
Newhaven	32
Ninette	40
Ostrich	26
Rendlesham	14
Rewga	36
Richmond	38
River Leven	37
River Tummel	37
Rochester	23, 36
Saxmundham	22, 33
Scarborough	21
Shamrock	32
Thistle	28
Valentia	33
Valeria	3
Vanessa Ann	65
Walsingham	20
William Harrison	29
Witham	37, 42
Wolseley	14
Yulan	24
Zonia	16

FISHING NEWS
25th February 1955

Trawling Firm Up-anchor in Lowestoft

CONSOLIDATED Fisheries Ltd., are to close their Lowestoft branch after 34 years at the port. This was announced by their Lowestoft manager, Mr. Long, who said: "The directors have decided to transfer Vanessa Ann, our latest diesel trawler, to Grimsby and to lay up the rest of our vessels operating out of Lowestoft."

Besides Vanessa Ann, the firm has been working seven older steam trawlers out of the port. Between the wars the firm had as many as 38 trawlers at Lowestoft. They first sent trawlers there towards the end of the first world war and opened a branch in 1921.

Reproduced by kind permission of Mr. Tim Oliver, Editor of Fishing News.

BACK COVER PHOTOGRAPHS

(Left) Built as *H383* in 1897 by A. Hall at Aberdeen, the *City of Aberdeen* became *LT326* in 1927. After a number of changes in ownership, she was sold for scrapping in 1950. *City of Aberdeen* is seen here in the 1930s off Lowestoft. As with a number of photographs in this book, this print has been supplied by the copyright owners Maritime Photo Library. (Right) This fine view, taken from South Pier, shows the *Bellerophon* after being sold by the Company. She was transferred by Consolidated to Lowestoft in 1920, and for the next eight years carried her Grimsby registration of *GY335*. During 1928, *Bellerophon* became *LT396,* and in 1946 was sold to Milford Haven. During April 1954, she was sold for scrapping.